The Wonderful Counselor

Tina Porter

The Wonderful Counselor

Counseling and Therapy with Jesus

The One Who Heals and Restores Mind, Body, Soul, and Spirit

Tina Porter, M.A. QMHP, B.S.W.
Christian Counselor and Psychotherapist
Trauma, Grief, Mental Health Expert, Pastor, and Prophetess

Inspire Hope Publishing™
"Books That Inspire Hope"
Inspire Hope Counseling Ministry Center, LLC

The Wonderful Counselor

Counseling and Therapy with Jesus

The One Who Heals and Restores Mind, Body, Soul, and Spirit

Published by Inspire Hope Publishing®, Marion, IL. 62959

www.inspirehopeministry.org

ISBN 979-8-218-76239-1

Edited by Tina Porter, Founder and Owner of Inspire Hope Publishing

and Inspire Hope Counseling Ministry Center, LLC

Formatted by Shelley Wilburn, Mountain Joy Publishing and Walking Healed Ministries

Front Cover Design by Tina Porter and Aidan Fusco

Cover Designs and Photography by Aidan Fusco Creative Studios

Cover Graphics courtesy of Canva

Printed in the United Stated of America

What People Are Saying About "The Wonderful Counselor"

"Mrs. Porter skillfully bridges the natural and the supernatural while offering insight from her decades of experience. Her calling as a prophetic counselor is evident from beginning to end."

~Dr. Clinton J Mohr, MD

"Tina Porter's book, *The Wonderful Counselor* is a timely and powerful resource for anyone seeking true healing—mentally, emotionally, and spiritually. As someone who was deeply impacted by her first book, *Pain to Purpose*, I was eager to dive into her second work, and it did not disappoint. In Pain to Purpose, Tina shared her personal journey through grief and how the Holy Spirit brought her into healing and victory. Through her transparency and Spirit-led prayers, I found myself returning to Jesus in a deeper way.

In *The Wonderful Counselor*, Tina once again brings a message of hope—this time highlighting the vital role of the Holy Spirit as our ever-present helper. With grace and clarity, she unpacks the connection between spirit, soul, and body, making complex concepts both understandable and relatable. What sets this book apart is her unique ability to blend scientific understanding of mental health with biblical truth. It's rare—and refreshing—to see a counselor who can bridge both worlds with such wisdom and authority.

As a chiropractor and natural health practitioner, I especially appreciate Tina's insight into how spiritual discernment can guide the healing process. I've witnessed in my own practice how the Holy Spirit can reveal root issues more quickly than conventional methods alone. Tina's book affirms this truth and encourages professionals in every healing field—be it counseling, medicine, or natural therapy—to listen with spiritual ears.

The Wonderful Counselor is more than a book—it's a tool for transformation. Whether you're a professional in the healing arts or someone walking through your own healing journey, this book will reassure you that you are not alone. You have a Helper—and He is wonderful indeed.

~Dr. Jason and Dr. Bobbie Whitacre, D.C., Doctor of Chiropractic Murphysboro Chiropractic and Wellness Doctor of Chiropractic Specializing in Functional Nutrition and Weight Loss

"While mental health has been ushered into the spotlight in recent years, there is still such a stigma about both mental health and counseling among Christian circles. In *The Wonderful Counselor*, Mrs. Porter artfully removes the blindfold from the church's mindset on not only the acceptable nature of counseling for Christians, but the absolute necessity of it. A fascinating read that will shake up the often conventional but dangerous view of mental health among believers. We highly recommend!"

~ Brandi & Chris Futrell, hosts of Prime Marriage Podcast, Author of The Journey: Staying on the Path

Reading *The Wonderful Counselor* is like sitting in the presence of someone who sees your pain, honors your story, and gently reminds you that you are never alone in it. Tina writes with the tenderness of a mother, the insight of a seasoned counselor, and the kind of faith that's been tested by heartbreak and still chooses hope.

As someone who has the privilege of calling Tina my cousin, though she's always felt more like an older sister, I've witnessed her profound journey firsthand. After experiencing unimaginable loss, she chose to let grief become the beginning for something deeply healing and redemptive. This book is the outpouring of that journey. It's not a manual, it's a ministry of love, hope, and healing.

Tina bridges the gap between psychology and faith with wisdom and compassion. She speaks to the impact of trauma with clinical clarity, then gently invites readers to find rest in God who comforts, counsels, and heals. As a licensed therapist who no longer practices but now works in behavioral health operations, I'm deeply moved by how seamlessly she weaves mental health education with spiritual truth. My clinical foundation was rooted in helping people understand their relationships, to themselves, to others, and to the mental health challenges they face. I truly value the way Tina places connection, both with God and with others, at the center of authentic healing. I see this book as an invaluable resource, not only for those seeking healing, but for new and seasoned clinicians committed to offering care that integrates clinical insight with spiritual depth. It's the kind of work that helps raise the standard of care across every level of our field.

The Wonderful Counselor is for anyone navigating sorrow, longing for peace, or trying to make sense of the ache in their soul. Whether you're a believer seeking spiritual guidance or someone in emotional pain just trying to get through the day, this book offers both practical insight and holy reassurance. Tina's words remind us that healing is possible, that Jesus is close to the brokenhearted, and that faith and therapy are not opposing paths, but deeply connected and mutually reinforcing.

I'm so proud of you, Tina. You've put your whole heart into this book, and I know it will bring comfort and hope to so many. The love and light of your son, Aaron Jr., "AP3" shines through every word; you carry him with you in the most beautiful way.

With love always,

~ Vanessa Granger-Belcher, M.S., LCPC, LMHC
LifeStance Health | Operations Strategy

I have the privilege to be the daughter of Tina Porter, the author of *The Wonderful Counselor*. As a Mental Health Clinician/Therapist, I specialize in Cognitive Behavioral Therapy and trauma-focused therapy. I work closely with children, youth, and families of different backgrounds. I see firsthand how adverse childhood experiences and trauma affects the mind, body, and spirit and how healing can unfold through both therapeutic and spiritual pathways.

The Wonderful Counselor is a profound and compassionate exploration of how trauma impacts individuals, how faith can anchor us, and how healing is truly possible. With wisdom, compassion, and professionalism, Tina Porter weaves together psychological insight and spiritual truth. Tina offers hope to anyone on the journey towards wholeness.

This book can remind others that God is present even in our darkest moments, and that healing mentally, emotionally, and spiritually is not only possible but promised. I encourage individuals to read this book because it is an essential read for anyone walking through pain or walking with others through it.

~ Jaidyn Hannah Porter, M.S.W, QMHP, B.S.W. Mental Health Clinician-Therapist Stress & Trauma Treatment Center, Inc. Respectfully, Daughter of Tina Porter, Author of "The Wonderful Counselor"

Table of Contents

Come to Jesus All Who Are Heavy Burdened and Find Rest!

Come to Me, all you who labor and are heavy laden, and I will give you rest. ~ **Matthew 11:28**

"...And His name will be called Wonderful Counselor, Mighty God, Everlasting Father, Prince of Peace." ~ Isaiah 9:6 (NKJV)

Be enlightened as Tina Porter shines the light on mental health, breaking the stigma and misconception on mental health related issues, mental disorders, and faith. Tina gives professional insight as a Qualified Mental Health Professional and as a Christ-Centered Psychotherapist, spiritual guidance as it relates to Christian Faith Values and Beliefs. As a Pastor, Minister, and Prophetic Counselor of the Christian Faith, Tina also gives Biblical insight regarding the importance of stewarding mental health integrating the Christian Faith, Psychology, and Spirituality. As an Author, she takes the reader on a journey to understand how Jesus walks with us and talks with us when faced with trauma, grief, crisis, mental, and emotional distress. Jesus is clearly depicted as *The Wonderful Counselor*. Tina helps the reader to understand that Counseling is ordained by God and *The Spirit of Counsel* is one of the attributes and functions of

God.

Tina emphasizes on how traumatic events that occurred in a significant developmental stage of the human life span development can disrupt a healthy development leading to mental disorders, physiological issues, unhealthy behavioral patterns, psychological, and emotional distress. Tina discusses maladaptive behaviors and how these behaviors are associated with inability to cope with complex life changes associated with adverse situations and adverse childhood experiences. Tina helps the reader to understand how unprocessed trauma and difficult circumstances can cause social, cognitive, and behavioral deficits. Tina explains how effective open and honest communication enhances closeness in relationships, promotes healing, fosters trust, provides validation, and empathy. Jesus is seen clearly throughout the book as being empathetic, nurturing, and consoling.

As a Mental Health, Trauma, Grief Expert, and Counselor/Therapist, Tina shares her expertise on understanding patterns of irrational thinking or cognitive distortions that contribute to unhealthy behavioral patterns. Tina explains how these distorted thought patterns can affect how one views themselves, the world, life, other people, and relationships. Tina proclaims that Jesus is the *Prince of Peace*, *The Way, The Truth, and the Life*. Jesus is described throughout the book, as *Healer, Comforter, The God of Hope and Restoration.* Tina connects the reader to experience the presence and love of God, by her transparency and written prayers.

Tina prophesies directly to the reader as to what God is personally saying to each person who reads this book, *The Wonderful Counselor*.

Dedication

I dedicate this book to all those who are in the helping and healing profession. I dedicate this book to Pastors, Ministers, Christian Counselors, Pastoral Counselors, Biblical Counselors, Church Lay Leaders, Ministry Leaders, Chaplains, Human Service Providers, Non-Licensed Counselors, Psychotherapists, Mental Health Coaches, Life Coaches, Qualified Mental Health Professionals, Licensed Professional Counselors, Licensed Clinical Professional Counselors, Licensed Mental Health Counselors, Licensed Marriage and Family Therapists, Licensed Clinical Social Workers, Licensed Social Workers, Psychologists, Psychiatrists, Psychiatric Nurse Practitioners, Medical Doctors, Medical Professionals, and other Mental Health Practitioners.

Your work is highly important and valuable. As you serve on the frontline daily helping those in need, never forget the reason why you made the decision to do the work that you do. I encourage you all to allow the gift of compassion that you have to be the driving force as you continue to serve the many clients, patients, church members, community members, and all the people that you help on a regular basis. I encourage you all to be full of empathy and love valuing every single person that seeks your care as you help others heal and excel on this journey of life. You are an *"Agent of Hope, Change, and Healing."* You are important, appreciated, valued, and noticed by God, the Creator of the Universe. I inspire you to allow God's love to permeate through you and flow out of you in the work that you do.

I would also like to dedicate this book to all those who have suffered emotionally, mentally, physically, and spiritually in this life. I dedicate this book to all the many trauma survivors who experienced some sort or level of trauma, and to all the victims of abuse and violence. I want to encourage you as you read this book to allow the love of God to penetrate your heart, let go of all that has oppressed you, and allow the healing power of God to do what has been impossible for man but is truly possible for God!

Most importantly, I dedicate this book to my Lord, Savior, and King, Jesus who has personally demonstrated His unrelenting love, mercy, and grace to me in every challenging season in my life. When I was in the valley you were there, when I was on the mountaintop you were there! You have been my hope and anchor! You are my confidant, my comforter, my strength, my healer, *Everlasting Father*, and my *Wonderful Counselor*!

I inspire you to embrace hope and encourage you to let *Hope* arise!

Acknowledgements

I want to acknowledge my Heavenly Father, God who is *Jehovah Rapha*, our *Healer*! My Father who has been with me every step throughout my journey of life. He has showed me who I am in Him, and that, I will forever be grateful for. When I didn't understand why I faced so many adversities throughout the different periods in my life you walked with me patiently. You taught me what I needed to learn in seasons of trials and tribulations. When my faith was tested, you never let me go. Instead, you believed in me, and undergirded me with your strength. You covered me with your grace and mercy. You guided me with your precious Holy Spirit. You gave me wisdom, revelatory insight, understanding, and peace that surpassed my understanding. I couldn't have written and published the two books, *"Pain to Purpose,"* and *"The Wonderful Counselor"* following a very difficult season of despair, grief, loss, trauma, and tragedy in 2018 without my God!

I am forever grateful to my Lord and Savior, Jesus Christ who took me by my hand and guided me through the suffering. Jesus personally helped me navigate through trauma and grief. For His purpose, I will reciprocate to others the compassion, hope, and counsel that He has given me on my journey of healing. I will be His conduit for His awesome healing power and Spirit to operate through all for His Glory and the revealing of His Kingdom to be established on earth as it is in Heaven throughout the world!

I acknowledge my Pastors, Jason and Melissa McKinnies, and the entire Purpose House Church Family who has supported, prayed, and believed in the Ministry and business of Inspire Hope Counseling Ministry Center, LLC housed at Purpose House Church to be a catalyst for REVIVAL! I have witnessed the God of hope resurrect people out of their despair. I have witnessed healing, reconciliation, restoration, salvation, minds transformed, and renewal in the lives of countless of people. I have been given a great opportunity and mandate to serve several thousands of people across the Southern Illinois Region thus far, and virtually in other states introducing them to the *Great Healer, Jesus, The Wonderful Counselor* allowing people to encounter His love and resurrecting power!

I also want to acknowledge my family who has been my greatest support! I forever love you, my husband, Pastor Aaron Porter Sr., my daughter's Jasmine, Jaidyn, Alayna, my beloved son, Aaron Joseph Porter, Jr. "AP3" who is watching from Heaven and cheering me on to fulfill heaven's plan and purpose on earth, and my amazing grandsons, Easton and Arrington who were sent to me as gifts from Heaven to inspire me to keep persevering. I love you for an eternity! To all my extended family and friends who love and support me, I acknowledge you and I love you beyond words! I am forever grateful and appreciative of you and all that you do for me and my family.

Professional Acknowledgements

Professional Clinical, Medical, Psychological, and Scientific Resources and Cited Work of Provided Information in the Book, The Wonderful Counselor

As the Author of *The Wonderful Counselor,* I acknowledge and appreciate all the great psychological researchers, scientists, medical and mental health professionals, and authors who have studied and proven efficacy of treatment for psychological issues, neurobiological, and physiological ailments, that I discuss, highlight, and write about in this book.

I acknowledge the clinical work, and studies that has proven efficacy for the treatment and psychological therapy of people who suffer from mental health disorders, mental illnesses, trauma, grief, psychological and emotional distress.

I would like to acknowledge all the provided medical, mental health, psychiatric, psychological, scientific terminology, verbiage, various diagnoses, data, summary, and paraphrased information of achieved work, findings, and statistical findings that I provide in this book that are acknowledged, and referenced in the back of the book in the ***Endnotes*** sequentially numbered in consecutive order per chapter listed as professional clinical resource cited work of comprehensive sources used.

Preface

An Invitation to The Wonderful Counselor

Note from the Author, Tina Porter: I invite you to read the Prophetic Message from God to you to embrace who Jesus truly is as *The Wonderful Counselor.*

I know where you are today. I've seen all what has happened in your life. Even when you didn't know that I was there. When you experienced the hardship, I was there. I have walked alongside of you in every season of your life. In every experience whether good or bad, I was right there by your side.

I gave you strength when you didn't have the strength to carry on. I comforted you when all alone, distraught, and the tears rolled from your eyes down your face. I've captured every tear and kept it concealed. The tears that I have collected are not forgotten. I value your tears. I value you far and beyond all who has been and is part of your life.

You are the *apple of my eye*. I cherish and protect you. You are so precious and valuable to me. Just as the pupil is the delicate and vital part of the eye so are you. I will carefully protect you even when you have felt that I have let you down or did not protect you. The sufferings you faced were never meant to destroy you rather they were to develop you. It is in the suffering when you encounter my tangible presence. Just as I too suffered in my humanity, I share in your suffering. It is in our shared suffering that connects us.

To share in My suffering here in this life is to also share in My Glory. At the appointed time you will experience the glory that will be revealed to you and

everything that you endured in this life. Every tear you've sown will reap an unending joy and victory.

I encourage you to hold on to the *Eternal Hope* that I have promised you and you will find rest for your soul.

~ ***Jesus***

Foreword

In her book, *The Wonderful Counselor*, Tina Porter integrates the power of Christian spirituality with Christian counseling to successfully overcome severe trauma and build healthy lives. Porter provides extensive Biblical scripture outlining how Jesus heals. As well, through Christian counseling based on well-documented psychological principles and therapy interventions, she explains how we can restore and build a satisfying and productive life.

A woman of profound Christian faith, Tina Porter is a Christian Counselor who has trained as a Cognitive Behavioral Therapist specializing in the treatment of severe trauma and family dysfunction. She is not an author writing to us from a personal distance. Instead, she uses her personal trauma and life journey growing in her faith and building her counseling skills and knowledge to illustrate her message. Her son, a wonderful young man and college athlete, died in a traffic accident in his third year of college. She and her family were devastated feeling hopeless.

As she addresses in the book, God does not always answer our prayers on our timeline but stays with us through the healing process. Moreover, she states that we must be proactive in our own healing as well as using prayer. As she states repeatedly, we need both.

This book is the end result of enormous research and integration of Biblical and psychological knowledge to help us recover and lead lives with good relationships, hope, and peace. I applaud Tina Porter and I am awestruck by this tremendous undertaking and accomplishment!

~ Dr. Brenda Gilbert, Ph.D., Clinical Psychologist

Second Foreword

Perspective on Mental Health & Faith

For too long, the conversation around mental health within many church communities has been shrouded in silence, misunderstanding, and, at times, outright denial. Though the church is called to be a place of healing and refuge, mental health struggles have often been seen as a sign of weak faith, spiritual failure, or even personal sin. In *The Wonderful Counselor* Tina dismantles the long overdue stigma.

The reality is simple: mental health is a part of human health. Just as we tend to broken bones or chronic illnesses, we must also care for our emotional and psychological well-being. Scripture is filled with examples of people grappling with depression, anxiety, fear, and despair—Elijah's exhaustion and hopelessness, David's cries of anguish in the Psalms, and even Jesus' deep emotional, psychological, and physical distress in the Garden of Gethsemane. These stories remind us that experiencing mental and emotional struggles does not make anyone less faithful or less loved by God.

Churches must recognize that prayer and faith are not in opposition to therapy, medication, or mental health support. In fact, they can work hand-in-hand. God has gifted people with wisdom and skills in counseling, psychology, psychiatry, and the practice of medicine for the very purpose of healing. To reject those tools is to reject part of the grace God offers through others.

Equally important is equipping the church with practical resources, and partnering with Christian counselors, offering support groups, and training leaders in mental health.

Ultimately, the church must remember its core calling: to be a place of compassion, grace, and healing. Breaking the stigma of mental health isn't just about addressing a social issue—it's about living out the Gospel. It's about seeing every person as loved by God, worthy of dignity and care for mind, body, soul, and spirit.

Faith and mental health are two deeply personal aspects of human life, each shaping the way people navigate challenges, pain, and purpose. While historically, these spheres have sometimes been viewed in tension—faith communities might emphasize prayer over therapy, or mental health professionals might sideline spirituality—there is growing recognition that both can coexist, compliment, and even enrich each other. In *The Wonderful Counselor*, every page paints a beautiful picture of how mental health and faith can co-exist.

~ *Aaron J. Porter Sr., Pastor and Mental Health Coach*

Introduction

Mental Health is a vital part of our human existence. The brain is the engine of our physical body. Therefore, brain health is very important. The Spirit is the core of who we are that contribute to our brain the personalities, creative abilities, innovations, and so much more all to be used for the glorification of our God, the Creator of the Universe, and all living things. Thoughts, feelings, and behaviors are interconnected (Beck, 1976).

Soul care involves tending to the mind, emotions, and spirit that fosters inner peace, and leads to a fulfilling life. Whole-person care is very instrumental in having a balance in mind, body, soul, and spirit. We cannot neglect the stewardship of caring for all four components in which God has entrusted to us. We have one body that we receive while living on this earth. It is our responsibility to care for our body because our physical bodies belong to God. Our bodies are the living breathing temple of the Living God. We are to take care of our physical bodies with great respect, dignity, and seriousness so that we may glorify God with our body. While we occupy the body that was created for our spirit to inhabit in this life on earth it is crucial that we understand how to care for the various multidimensional aspects of our existence.

In this book, *The Wonderful Counselor* you will learn that not everything we struggle with in this life is spiritual but is also psychological and physiological. We are spiritual, emotional, social, psychological, and physical beings. Since we live in a fallible world this life is perishable and temporal. Circumstances will arise that will cause mental and emotional distress that is a normal human response. Physiological, emotional, psycho-social, and psychological responses to trauma, grief, loss, and crisis are inevitable. However, Jesus, *The Wonderful Counselor* meets us in these times of afflictions and shares in our humanity. Jesus consoles us, empathizes with us, and by His Holy Spirit comforts us. Jesus gives peace that overrides our natural understanding, provides joy that is unexplainable, gives us hope that anchors our souls, and healing that establishes us.

Adverse Childhood Experiences (Felitti et al., 1998) are early root systems that can lead to detrimental mental and behavioral disorders as an adult that cripple the spirit of a person. However, God created the mind to heal and has given the brain the ability to be restructured. With God all things are possible. God provides strategies and tools as healing agents. God calls, equips, and anoints people to serve as conduits for His healing power and Spirit to operate through. He chooses who will be used as His instrument to deliver His healing, reconciliation, and restoration to the distressed, hurting, broken, battered, sick, and lost. In Jesus, one can find rest for the soul if they choose to come to Him and receive His healing power and virtue. Above all else, God wants the spirit of man and woman to be free from any tie or bond that holds them in captivity. God liberates people by the *Spirit of Counsel.* Counseling is a gift from God to connect all who are weary and heavy laden to Jesus who took the burdens for us so that we may live in peace, freedom, and in eternal hope. Open your heart and mind as you discover how Jesus heals and restores mind, body, soul, and spirit.

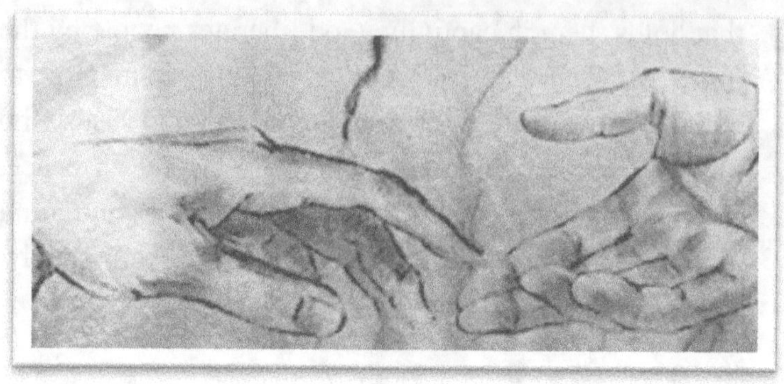

Chapter 1: The Spirit of Counsel

The spirit of the LORD will rest on Him--the Spirit of wisdom and of understanding, the Spirit of counsel and of might, the Spirit of the knowledge and fear of the LORD," – Isaiah 11:2, NIV.

God had you on His mind before time! The Father's plan has always been to meet you where you are, to console, comfort, and embrace you with His pure love. God desires to be relatable and relational. Most importantly, God wants to be your confidant. God, the Father, the Creator of the universe and all creation ordained for His authority, kingship, reign, sovereignty, government, rulership, and dominion to rest; settle on Jesus the Messiah, the Christ, the Anointed One, God's only begotten son, God, who is spirit manifested in the flesh for all to encounter the *Wonderful Counselor.*

Jesus comes to save that which is lost, not to condemn, nor judge but to save that which is of the world. ***"For God, did not send His Son into the world to condemn the world, but in order that the world might be saved through Him." – John 3:17, NKJV***. Jesus is driven with compassion to meet you right where you are. God loved you first and for that reason, He seeks you out when you are lost on the journey of life. God pursues us in love not in judgement or condemnation. Jesus said, in John 12:47, *If anyone hears me and doesn't obey me, I am not his judge--for I have come to save the world not to judge it.* ***"For God so loved the world that He gave His only begotten Son, that whosoever believeth in Him should not perish, but have everlasting life." – John 3:16, NIV.***

To understand who God is and the vitality of how God functions you must first understand the existence, purpose, and movement of God's electromagnetic power that physically interacts with His creation on earth. The spiritual frequencies that flow from His throne in Heaven into the earth realm. ***"And from the throne proceeded lightnings, thunderings, and voices." – Revelation 4:5, NKJV.***

"In front of the throne, seven lamps of fire blazing before the throne, which are the seven Spirits of God." – Revelation 4:5. The earth is God's footstool meaning that the earth lays underneath the throne of God.

"Heaven is My throne, and earth is My footstool." – Isaiah 66:1, NKJV. The sevenfold Spirit of God is mentioned in Isaiah 11:2, which are *The Spirit of the Lord, The Spirit of wisdom, The Spirit of understanding, The Spirit of counsel, The Spirit of might, The Spirit of knowledge, and The Spirit of reverential fear of the Lord,* a feeling of deep respect, love, and awe as God being sacred. The nature and character of God is exemplified through Jesus. The sevenfold Spirit of God are manifested in Jesus. Jesus then demonstrated the manifestation of God's Spirit on earth as He demonstrated His ministry among man all the way up until the crucifixion where He demonstrated His unfailing and undeserving love for us through His sacrifice which became our eternal hope.

God desires all of us to obtain wisdom and understanding. As a matter of fact, we as human beings, were created to process information as to what we see, hear, feel, and experience in this life on earth. Our physical brain is created to organize thoughts, regulate emotions, process conscious experiences—feelings, and put everything we experience into healthy perspective. I often say to my clients during counseling and therapy sessions, that we must allow our brains to function the way it was created to function. The brain needs to obtain understanding, meaning, closure, and inner peace on an ongoing basis as we journey in this life that is full of good and bad experiences that effect our view about life, ourselves, and others. ***"Wisdom is the principle thing; Therefore, get wisdom. And in all your getting, get***

understanding." – Proverbs 4:7, NKJV.

God teaches us in the Bible, His Holy Word, that we are to share with other believers our burdens, that which is troublesome or too hard to cope with. ***"Carry each other's burdens, and in this way, you will fulfill the Law of Christ." – Galatians 6:2, NIV.*** The fulfillment of the *Law of Christ* is walking in love, and ***"There is no fear in love. But perfect love drives out fear, because fear has to do with punishment…" (1 John 4:18, NIV)***. God is more concerned with giving you space and time to openly share your struggles with someone rather than reprimanding you. Therefore, there is no need to fear about sharing your personal issues with a confidant that God has appointed in your life who gives you wise counsel. The *Spirit of Counsel* purposely comforts you in the time of hardship, anguish, and distress allowing you to be real with your thoughts, feelings, and experiences. God listens and empathizes with you. The *Spirit of Counsel* leads you on the path that God has destined for you, to give you direction and instruction.

God wants us to experience compassion, tenderness, love, community, shared humanity, emotional vulnerability, and support as obedience to Christ. This is the fulfillment of the Law of Christ. We are called to be *Imitators of Christ*, *Joint Heirs with Christ* and *Ambassadors of Christ* to carry on the ministry of Jesus by fulfilling everything He teaches us to establish the Kingdom of God on earth as it is in Heaven (Matthew 6:10). Jesus is love, God is love and we are commanded by Jesus to love one another just as Jesus loves us which brings healing to the human soul (John 13:34-35). Jesus gives us the *greatest commandment*, ***"...Love the Lord your God with all your heart and with all your soul and with all your mind.' This is the first and greatest commandment. And the second is like it: 'Love your neighbor as yourself." – Matthew 22:37-39, NIV.***

"Above all love each other deeply, because love covers a multitude of sins." – 1 Peter 4:8, NIV.

True healing, restoration, and reconciliation comes from receiving the love of the Father and reciprocating that love to others. When we do this, we allow Jesus to be seen through us and we become His true followers and disciples. Jesus tells us that the world will know us as His true disciples when we demonstrate love for one another (John 13:35). God as our Creator is showing us that we are relational beings because we are created in the *image of God* (Genesis 1:27).

God is relational, He desires to commune and fellowship with us daily. For this purpose, God created man in the beginning for fellowship and communion. However, when Adam and Eve lost that privilege because of disobedience allowing the enticement of their own will and desire to abandon the commands of God this communion was disrupted. This is why God, the Father in His love and mercy re-established a new precedent. God gave us direct access to Him directly through Jesus being the *Door* (John 10:9). He is the way, the truth, and the life. No one comes to the Father except through the son, Jesus (John 14:6). He loved us so much that what the first created man, Adam allowed Satan to sabotage, God restored!

In Jesus, God, the Father gave us, mankind, access to come to God boldly at His mercy seat by grace that was given to us at the atonement on the cross of Calvary where Jesus fulfilled His divine ordained purpose of God the Father. Jesus' divine purpose was to redeem mankind from eternal damnation through the sacrificial blood that was shed for all of us. The blood that blots out our sin and for us to obtain direct fellowship with God and have eternal hope by the righteousness of Jesus Christ. We become righteous through Jesus Christ. God is Holy. In order to commune with God, we too must come to Him through holiness and righteousness as we are found in Christ Jesus!

He is a righteous and just God who puts things in order to establish precedents for generations and for His Kingdom. God's decrees and statutes are established to solidify His plans and purposes. God is omniscient and omnipotent. He is the God of *all-knowing* and He is the *all-powerful* God who knew before time what would transpire. God had a plan for what was to come to change the trajectory of that which He created for His Glory and pleasure. God created mankind to have sons and daughters in order to have direct fellowship and communion with them. This is why God created Adam and Eve in the beginning before the fall of man, which Adam and Eve brought on earth. Due to the fall of man, the world became fallible.

God is love, hope, and peace. It is always the plan of God for us, His creation, to come into the full knowledge of who He is. To be adopted as His Sons and Daughters that only comes by believing in Jesus, accepting Jesus Christ as Lord and Savior, and baptized in water as a symbolic act of being reborn. Redeemed by the bloodshed of Jesus and the washing away of our sins through the sacrificial offering of Jesus at the Cross of Calvary. Then, coming into the relationship with the Father, Son, and Holy Spirit. Notice, I said coming *into relationship* and not coming into religion. Relationship, just as in any healthy relationship that we have requires consistent open honest communication, time, energy, investment, trust, accountability, cooperation, collaboration, and mutual agreement. That is what God wants from us more than anything. This requires surrendering our hearts, rendering what we think is right in our own eyes or what we desire rather than what God desires. The act of surrender is what allows you to receive the *Spirit of Counsel* in your life. As you receive the counsel of God your life will begin to prosper the way God intended.

It is God's Will that we renew our minds with what God has proclaimed in His Word, the Holy Bible in which Jesus became the *Living Word* to live and dwell among us here on earth. Jesus came to fulfill the Word. We are to be transformed into the same image as Jesus and allow God's Spirit to regenerate our hearts, growing in Christlikeness. ***"For whom He foreknew, He also predestined to be conformed to the image of His Son,***

that he might be the firstborn among many brothers." – Romans 8:29, NKJV. God wants us to be *doers of His Word and not just hearers of His Word* (James 1:22-25).

Emulating Jesus and being conformed to His likeness allow for Jesus to be manifested in us. We too receive the sevenfold Spirit of God that flows from the Throne of God in Heaven to all who inhabits earth in Christ who are in a right spiritual posture to receive the Spirit of the Lord, wisdom, understanding, counsel, might, knowledge, and fear/respect for God. There is nothing more valuable than to have the full operation of God's Spirit and the essence of who He is dwelling in you and flowing out of you to a dry and thirsty land in an imperfect world where suffering, loss, and trauma occur daily. In this imperfect world that we live in, people grow weary, hopeless, and mentally ill. God uses His willing vessels who are yielded to Him to reach the hurting and the hopeless.

When we are yielded to God allowing His Spirit to operate in us, only then, will those in need have an encounter with Jesus. The hurting will receive the goodness of Jesus, the *Living Water* who brings abundant life, nourishment, healing, and wholeness. As a Christian Counselor, a Master's Degree Level Psychotherapist, and Qualified Mental Health Professional, I have witnessed this firsthand in my 28-plus years of working in the helping profession and currently in my Christian counseling/therapy private practice, *Inspire Hope Counseling Ministry Center, LLC.* I have seen how Jesus reaches people where I could not in my own strength, intellect, and abilities by just simply yielding to Him. Allowing His Spirit to operate through me, and activating the gifts of the Holy Spirit within me that releases a divine flow of healing virtue to those in need. Some of these gifts as described in 1 Corinthians 12:8-10 include, *word of wisdom, word of knowledge, faith, gifts of healing, the power to do miracles, the ability to prophesy, and discern spirits…*

According to Romans 12:6-8, there are also gifts that include, prophecy which is to prophesy in proportion to our faith, ministry- to minister to others, and to teach others by giving them revelatory insight. The gift to give encouragement, diligently helping and leading others to become a better version of themselves that mirror God. Other gifts involve supporting others by serving them, showing mercy, contributing by giving generously of your time, energy, thoughts, resources, and administering. As well as to serve others by coming to where they are currently in their walk of life to accommodate their needs.

God has also appointed speaking gifts which are used as God's mouthpiece. These speaking gifts are, Apostles, Prophets, Evangelists, Teachers, and Pastors who often operate in the gift of exhortation, which is to empathetically encourage or urge someone to do something as God instructs (Ephesians 4:11). As well as, to provide comfort, reassurance, to correct in love when someone is stuck in a pattern of error that may be destructive to them, others, and their life. Finally, the speaking gifts are to lead others in truth. God is truth and so God commands those who have been appointed to operate in these giftings to walk in a spirit of truth helping others to think in a way that is true, noble, right, pure, lovely, admirable, excellent, and praiseworthy according to God (Philippians 4:8). When totally surrendered, devoted to God by submitting to His Lordship and hand of authority, only then can you truly operate as a joint heir with Jesus as His mouth, hands, and feet carrying on His ministry not your own.

The *Spirit of Counsel* as one of the *seven burning lamps* blazing as a flame of fire that stands before God's throne symbolizing light or illumination, a purging away or cleansing within you, as well as to produce warmth and comfort that envelopes you with the pure love that only comes from Abba, Father, God Himself. The very essence of God is love. ***"God is love, and whoever abides in love abides in God, and God abides in him. God is love, and all who live in love live in God, and God lives in them." – 1 John 4:16, NLT.*** Now that I have given you a foundation of the very essence of God, His nature, functionality, gifted vessels who He appoints to help people, and His purpose, let's explore how God connects with us in a way that revolutionizes us.

Again, God is Spirit. Therefore, He looks for physical bodies on earth to dwell in where His Spirit can flow freely through to reach people. God's agenda is always about souls and investing in people. People are His earthen treasure that He desires to mold and shape for eternal preparation. Take a moment and reflect about a time when you were in a dilemma or a crisis and there was someone who came to support and help you when you were in a time of need in some way. Whether it was a smile, a hug, nice gesture, act of kindness, shared words of encouragement, prayed with you or for you, and provided you with something that you needed at that given moment or time in your life. Now, ask yourself, how did you feel in that moment and during that period in your life? If you felt suddenly encouraged, loved, hopeful, peaceful, reassured, comforted, and strengthened, you encountered God. These are moments that you can guarantee are *God Moments,* or what I call *Messages from Heaven.* It's when God is letting you know that He is near, He sees you, knows, and understands what you are going through and steps out of eternity into the earth realm to meet you right in that moment or time period in response to your need.

God wink moments are God's way of letting you know that He loves you so much that He is willing to do whatever is necessary to let you know that He cares about every small or big detail of your life. God is the supplier of your needs and responds to what concerns you. ***"The Lord will perfect that which concerns me; Your mercy and loving-kindness, O Lord, endure forever-forsake not the works of Your own hands." – Psalms 138:8, AMPC.*** The funny thing about me writing this right now in this very moment, God decides to demonstrate what I am currently writing about that He most certainly is a God who responds to us when we are in dire need to solidify everything I am explaining. So, at my Private Practice, Inspire Hope Counseling

Ministry Center, LLC between my counseling sessions, I decide to take some time to write my book and a dilemma occurs in the women's bathroom where the toilet overflows and it is a mess in the last stall of the bathroom. I'm thinking to myself, *what am I going to do now*, I didn't want to bother the maintenance person at my church who was way on the other side of the church campus from where my counseling practice is located, and just like that, my husband shows up in a time of need and takes action to resolve the problem. This is how God operates. God knew my need and He put it on my husband's heart to drive to my practice and I was able to inform him on what happened, and he helped.

Now, you may say, well I have been in crisis situations or in a very difficult situation and I didn't understand why God didn't come to my immediate need? Perhaps, you even cried out to God, prayed in desperation, and so forth. Yet, no response. I have learned sometimes our perception is distorted as to how we perceive whether or not God responded to our need. God's response is not always the way we expect it. Often, the way God responds to our need doesn't come in the fashion we anticipated. The timing of His response may not be in alignment with what or how you envisioned. Our expectations can limit us from experiencing the blessing in how God responds. God is sovereign. Therefore, He knows what we need and how we need the aid that He provides for us in His timing. I recall singing in church years ago about God being right on time when you need Him the most. I've learned God may not always come when you want Him to, but He will always be right there in the nick of time. God is certainly an on-time God. God's timing is often not our timing.

As I indicated previously, God is an *All-Knowing* God, omniscient and omnipresent. God knows what is best. Because He sees things that we cannot. He is present everywhere in various times of our life. He is in the future just as much as He is in the now and has been in the past not only in our own lives but in the lives of others. God doesn't mean for the hardships that you encounter in this life to harm you but uses what has hurt you in some way to develop you. In other words, the suffering that you experience in this imperfect world is not meant to harm or destroy you. Rather, the suffering develops you. God will use trials of life to change your perception about life. God will allow growth and maturity during life tribulations to allow you to evolve into a better version of you. However, you have to be willing to undergo the process allowing God to shape and mold you.

God will use a tragedy that you may have personally experienced to promote growth in someone else. God sees a different masterpiece being created from His viewpoint that often supersedes our understanding. We can't see what God sees. We just simply trust that He knows best. God knows the outcome and what will transpire out of every negative circumstance just as well as in every positive situation that we face. God sees all the dots that need to be connected in order for something beautiful to be established. I see God as the master of artistry, the conductor of the orchestra, the great architect, the writer and author of so many stories that all point to Him being *Elohim*, the supreme and mighty God who holds the entire universe in His power, majesty, and glory!

God teaches us in Proverbs 3:5-6, that we are to *trust in God with all of our heart and not lean to our own understanding.* Yet, we are to acknowledge that He is God, ruler of Heaven and earth. With that being said, we know Him as the God who has all authority, dominion, and authorization for what happens to us all on earth. You may say, well how could God authorize such evil to occur, like murder, violence, abuse, loss, sudden tragedy, fatal illnesses, death, etc. As the *Spirit of Counsel* releases me to say; "It's not that God authorizes bad things to happen to us in this temporal life. God knows that this life is imperfect, and we live in a fallen world that is fallible with imperfect people inhabited on the earth."

Unfortunately, with imperfect people there comes poor choices as God has given mankind free-will to make choices. Sometimes, those bad choices hurt other people in the process. God also knows that great suffering will occur because again, the earth is fallible, and erroneous. The earth is full of error. This all came about after the fall of man in the beginning in the book of Genesis found in chapters 1-3 and how this falling world came about. Adam and Eve ate fruit off of the *Tree of Knowledge* of good and evil that God specifically, instructed them to not eat from. Man then, became mortal and no longer immortal as initially created in the divine form of God that was delightful, excellent, and *perfect*. The earth became perishable. Meaning, bad things are now bound to happen. Death and decay are now inevitable. But let us not forget, God always had a plan of redemption and salvation! This is the *good news*!

So, let's discuss further about the *Spirit of Counsel*. God equips us when the *Spirit of Counsel* is evident in a person who God appoints in your life. I often say, that when God appoints a person operating in this capacity of ministry in your life, it's because God is ready to speak directly to you. God is ready to help you to strategically develop, heal, grow, and mature. God does this because He is ready to prepare you for the destiny that He has called you to. I see it as an opportunity to change. Counseling is a birthing room preparing you for delivery. However, God is a gentleman. God will not force change on anyone who is not willing to withstand the process of transformation.

Those who do not trust God and His counsel often find it very difficult to trust the process that comes with the territory of counseling. What happens then, is the person(s) receiving counseling winds up aborting that which was appointed to be birthed. God nor the counselor that is operating in the *Spirit of Counsel* is responsible for your healing and transformation. You are responsible for healing by making a conscientious choice to begin the healing and recovery process. Contemplation of change is what is required. When you take the first step in acknowledging that I need to heal, recover, or get better then, Jesus takes you by the hand and walks this process with you. He does this by appointing His conduit of counsel and provides counseling through that person who has been anointed by God to serve in this capacity.

Let me encourage you, you can't help what's happened to you nor are you responsible for the trauma, grief, or crisis event that rocked your mental health in your life. However, you are responsible for taking steps to do your trauma, grief, and mental health work. It is important to not take it lightly when you have come in contact with someone who has been authorized by God to give you sound counsel. God ordained counseling. Counseling is a gift from God and He instructs us to seek counsel. Afterall, Jesus is *The Wonderful Counselor (Isaiah 9:6).*

"Where no counsel is, the people fall: But in the multitude of counselors there is safety." – Proverbs 11:14, KJV. People lose sight of direction not knowing the path that they should take when there is lack of understanding and knowledge about situations that may bring them to uncertainty. In fact, God indicates, ***"My people are destroyed for lack of knowledge. Because you have rejected knowledge, I will also reject you from being priest for Me; Because you have forgotten the law of your God, I also will forget your children." – Hosea 4:6, NKJV.***

There is protection in counseling. Why is that? Because sometimes our carnal sinful nature leads us astray by the way of our thinking that is often emotionally driven. If you are not spiritually nurtured or fed, you will be led by your emotions. I often say to my clients when providing counseling as the Holy Spirit leads me to, *it is very important to stop and think first before reacting*. When you take the time to pause and think first, ask yourself, are the thoughts that I am having true, is there any evidence to solidify truth, does this thought serve me and others well, are my current thoughts constructive? If not, then do not act upon the thoughts nor speak it out during a communication dialogue that may contribute to conflict or create non-productive communication, and a cycle of destructive communication. Moreover, I advise people to not allow the thoughts to linger and entertain your mind. You must be quick to dispel any thoughts that are non-constructive or even distorted. Think on the lines of being *responsive* rather than *emotionally reactive*.

God may sound harsh in the scripture passage, Hosea 4:6 that I referenced above. However, God is truth, and He speaks honestly to us in this scripture passage. It's the same concept of when a teacher is providing their students' knowledge, but they do not hear what the teacher is saying nor receiving what is being taught. The students are refusing to attain the knowledge. When it is time for a test, the students' will not be prepared for the test. More than likely, the students will fail. For that reason, the teacher cannot give them a passing grade that will now hinder achievement. In college, perhaps a student is needing a specific course in order to achieve their degree to obtain the professional occupation desired. Yet, the student doesn't give any effort towards obtaining the knowledge needed to pass the course. Refusing to read, study, prepare for tests and assignments will lead to failure. For that reason, the college professor can't pass the student. The professor doesn't see fit for the student to proceed in obtaining that particular professional role and deems them incompetent due to the lack of preparation.

God wants us to obtain knowledge that will give us stability. He has given us all a manual, the Holy Bible to guide us all that we may prosper in every area of our lives. Whether it's mentally, emotionally, spiritually, or physically. As well as in our finances, relationships, in a marriage, family, profession, and ministry. When we reject knowledge, we reap the consequences. Those consequences can be detrimental. In such cases, could be a loss of a marriage, family discord-dysfunction, financial difficulties, health issues, communication barriers, hinderance in ministry, loss of a job, mental health crisis, mental health disorders, and the list goes on.

The Word of God declares that we have the *mind of Christ,* and we are to *renew our minds daily.* We have the *mind of Christ* if we choose to bring our own unhealthy thought patterns under the subjection of Christ. Ephesians 4:23 (AMPC) says, ***"Be constantly renewed in the spirit of your mind [having a fresh mental and spiritual attitude]."***

Romans 12:2 states, ***"Do not be conformed to this world, but be transformed by the renewal of your mind, that by testing you may discern what is the will of God, what is good and acceptable and perfect."***

I love what **2 Timothy 2:15** (NIV) states, ***"Do your best to present yourself to God as one approved, a worker who does not need to be ashamed and who correctly handles the word of truth."***

Let's talk about thought patterns. Thought patterns are a habit of thinking in a consistent particular way, utilizing assumptions that derive from the interactions we have daily and momentarily in life. The cognition is so crucial for the human brain. Not everything is spiritual. A lot of times situations you are struggling with are psychological. We are spiritual beings yet, we are psychological, emotional, and physical beings. God wants us to be balanced in mind, body, spirit, and soul. *The Spirit of Counsel* is the interconnection between God and the person or vessel that is being used as a conduit for God. That person who is a conduit for God understands the *Mind of God.* They are conduits of God's Spirit to transfer the revelatory insight, knowledge, wisdom, strength, reverential fear, and admonishment to others they serve who provides foundational stability to function as a healthy, whole, and balanced triune being, mind, body, spirit the way God created us. God too, being a triune God who is one *being* functioning in three parts as the Father, Son, and Holy Spirit. Three biblically is the number that signifies the divine completion of God, and it represents perfection and bringing things into maturity or alignment. The Counsel of God is the lifeline for many. The *Spirit of Counsel* is the demonstration of God's resurrecting power that heals the mind, heart, soul, and spirit.

The *Spirit of Counsel* is the supernatural gift of the Holy Spirit to help people make right judgments and act in a way that brings glory to God. We are all given a free will to make personal judgement calls or choices in each situation by intuition. The *Spirit of Counsel* provides guidance, guiding you to defend the truths of your faith. The *Spirit of Counsel* gives you an opportunity to hear God speak through the people God puts in your life. The *Spirit of Counsel* helps you recognize the need to identify and neutralize destructive factors that hinder you in life. The *Spirit of Counsel* introduces new healthy, constructive, and positive elements into your life. Therefore, having tools to improve yourself, change thoughts, core beliefs, choices, and behavioral patterns. The *Spirit of Counsel* is a supernatural function that comes directly from God. The *Spirit of Counsel* tells us about God, reveals the frailty of man, the broken relationship between God and man, and how God made a way for the relationship to be restored. We have an obligation to recognize the need for our relationship with God to be restored and to posture ourselves spiritually to receive the Spirit of the Lord, wisdom, knowledge, counsel, His might, and reverence of God to excel in life.

According to the Bible, *The Spirit of Counsel* is the Holy Spirit in operation to guide and advise individuals to take the best course of action. The Holy Spirit essentially provides divine insight and wisdom that comes directly from God. The Spirit of Counsel gives the Counselor abilities who is functioning under the divine inspiration of God to discern God's Will in specific life situations influencing the individual to make righteous decisions. The *Spirit of Counsel* is a personal advisor providing divine inner guidance to help navigate through difficult decisions and circumstances. I recall on many occasions during a counseling/therapy session as a counselor listening to horrendous situations that are very overwhelming to hear and all of a sudden, I can hear God's voice so clearly telling me to speak precisely to what those individual needs are in the moment in order to help that person. Only God knows exactly what to say to an individual who is struggling.

As a counselor operating under the power of the *Spirit of Counsel*, I rely on God's Spirit to operate in me to bring true healing, deliverance, guidance, hope, reassurance, peace, and so much more. It's quite magnificent to witness the power of God in full operation. I can literally see the countenance of the person's face change and light up when God speaks. I can sense and see the heaviness and darkness lift off the person who is receiving counseling. God's Will executed as the *Spirit of Counsel* that is in full operation enables individuals to identify and discern what aligns with God's plans. The Counselor is gifted by the Holy Spirit to empower and lead people to take right action at the appropriate time. God gives clear instruction on what to do and not to do. The *Spirit of Counsel* is the third function of the sevenfold of God's Spirit in Isaiah 11:2. I do not believe that is coincidental. God intended for the *Spirit of Counsel* to be written out in order in the Bible on purpose in this particular scripture verse. Isaiah 11:2 profoundly describes the Messiah as the Godly leader of Israel, who will rise from the root of Jesse and King David who will reign as the Spirit of the Lord rest on Him to give him wisdom, understanding, counsel, power, knowledge, and the reverential fear of the Father, God.

The *Spirit of Counsel* is recorded in the scripture of Isaiah 11:2 as number "3," the *third function* of God's Spirit meaning that the three persons of the Trinity, functioning as God, the Father, Son, and Holy Spirit; sharing one divine nature existing eternally together who gives *Counsel* to bring things into complete divine wholeness, completion, and perfection in the lives of His people, which is the biblical meaning of the number "3". The number "3" also signifies growth and reproduction. God's intention is to always see fit that His people are growing spiritually. God reproduces Himself by sowing seeds of goodness and truth in the lives of His people that He gives counsel to. Then, those people will sow those seeds in the lives of others as this is part of God's divine plan as the eternal *Tree of Life* flourishes on earth as it is in Heaven. The Tree of Life mentioned in Genesis, Proverbs, Revelation, and other parts of The Holy Bible symbolizes the flow of life. God as the source of life who imparts His abundant life to humans. Then, those humans are to then give life to others and His creation.

This *Tree of Life* and this process of spiritual reproduction represents the overturning of the curse in which Adam and Eve experienced when they disobeyed God in Genesis 3 by eating the forbidden fruit from the *Tree of Knowledge* that brought sin and separation from God into the world. God is the God of Restoration! God is restoring His initial plan and purpose for the *Tree of Life* to once again be the center of His Kingdom as it initially was in the Garden of Eden. You see, this is why Jesus indicated in John 15:5 (KJV) that, ***"I am the vine, ye are the branches: He that abideth in me, and I in Him, the same bringeth forth much fruit: for without me ye can do nothing."*** The vine represents Jesus. The branches represent all of us who are believers, followers, and disciples of Jesus.

The Gardener represents God the Father who tends to the garden of life here on earth from Heaven always watching, pruning, and pulling out the weeds in the garden of our personal life that hinder us. God does this so that we will grow stronger, flourish, produce good and much more fruit in life in preparation for eternity. Abiding in Jesus means to stay connected to the vine for spiritual nourishment in order for you to bear fruit representing goodness in this life. This is why *The Spirit of Counsel* is a very important function of God's sevenfold spirit because this is how He keeps His people connected to Him. God, the Father wants us all to be grafted as "The Church" as a collective people of God in union as the *Olive Tree* (Romans 11:17) representing the Jews, the chosen people of God as the familial lineage of

Jesus and the Gentiles who are all those who are not Jewish who have received Jesus as Lord and Savior whom sins have been washed by the blood of Jesus through the sacrificial atonement of Jesus on the Cross of Calvary. You will be blessed as you heed to and open your mind to receive what God speaks to you through the *Spirit of Counsel.* When God speaks, He gives life. He is the peace giver. God gives you peace beyond your understanding. God convicts you when you're wrong and leads you into truth. He calms the storms that are raging in your life. God strengthens you and brings comfort, and as Psalms 3:3 declares, *He is the lifter of your head.* The Spirit of God casts out fear, alleviates anxiety, excessive worry, expels and replaces doubt with faith. God's spirit gives hope, reassurance, and encouragement. As you walk with Jesus you will experience the unfolding of spiritual prosperity that causes every other area of your life to prosper.

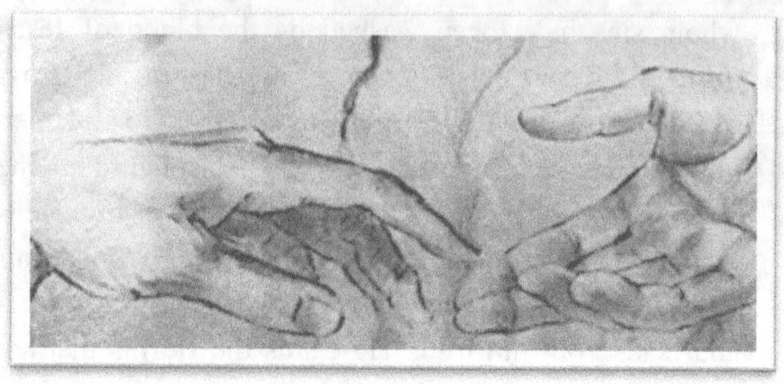

Chapter 2: Mental Health as Your Soul Prospers

"Beloved, I pray that you may prosper in all things and be in health, just as your soul prospers." – 3 John 1:2, NKJV

Mental Health is often neglected or carries a stigma. Especially, in the religious sector where often in the past, mental health issues are or have been looked at as a spiritual issue rather than a psychological issue. As a professional in the mental health sector and a Pastor in the church, I would like to shed light on this misconception and break the stigma. As a master's degree level counselor practicing Christ-centered mental health counseling, biblical counseling, a clinically trained psychotherapist/counselor, and founder/owner of a professional Christian faith-based counseling business, I am going to provide some insight on mental health. God has called me to lead a ministry as an agent of the Church, and a catalyst of hope to help restore mental health not only in the church but for the community as well. Mental Health is a major item on God's agenda. Throughout the years in the church, mental health issues and exposing emotional vulnerabilities are frowned upon and seen as being spiritually weak or not having enough faith if a person struggles with mental health issues. Mental health issues have been ignored for so long not only in the religious sector but just in general in society alone.

However, now, mental health is looked at more seriously with all that is going on in our society today; gun violence, wars, world health pandemic crisis, fatalities, humanitarian crisis, terrorism, hate crimes, economic crisis, political crisis, school shootings, racial unrest/divide, disparities, domestic and sexual violence, high divorce rates, opioid crisis, wars, and rumors of wars, and the list goes on. God is the God of restoration! It is His Will that people experience restorative health. God is Hope, and when the world seems hopeless, God brings hope in hopeless situations. When the world seems strangely dim and dark, God, who is the *Father of Lights* (James 1:17) comes to bring light through His sons and daughters who are willing vessels to be used by God for the edification of others who are hopeless. I love what James 1:17-18 (NKJV) states, ***"Every good gift***

and every perfect gift is from above, and comes down from the Father of lights, with whom there is no variation or shadow of turning. Of His own will He brought us forth by the word of truth, that we might be a kind of firstfruits of His creatures."

In actuality, if you consider what light does, it will help you understand the very nature of God. Light illuminates so one can see in the midst of darkness. For instance, when you are standing in a dark room, and someone brings a candle with a lit flame you can now see what you could not see prior to the light entering the room. Likewise, that is how it is with God. God is light and those who are His, having His Spirit residing within are *children of light*. ***1 Thessalonians 5:5 (ESV)*** states, ***"For you are all children of light, children of the day. We are not of the night or of the darkness." Ephesians 5:8 (NKJV)*** states, ***"For you were once darkness, but now you are light in the Lord. Walk as children of light."***

As we see now in our world times have changed drastically. There are times we don't even recognize our world due to so much calamity, destruction, unruly and inhumane behavior that often takes our breath away. We are sometimes taken aback, pausing, and questioning, *what in the world is going on*? As we look at biblical scripture, Jesus warns us that this world will grow dark as the time draws near when Jesus will return to the earth to gather up those who belong to God who have been redeemed by faith in Jesus Christ. So, as a believer in Christ, we mustn't be surprised about all the calamities we see in our world. Instead, we must position ourselves as to who God called us to be and that is to be messengers of hope, love, peace, and faith. God tells us in the *Day of the Lord,* that we are to *comfort* and *edify* others in the time of great trouble (1 Thessalonians 5:11). Again, remember, ***"You are all sons of light and sons of the day. We are not of the night nor of darkness." – 1 Thessalonians 5:5, NKJV.***

As sons and daughters of light we are to be vigilant and sober, always watching as darkness covers the earth to be ready to stand as a beacon of light.

As a Counselor having the *Spirit of Counsel* dwelling within, there is a responsibility and mandate of God to warn those who are unruly, those who lack discipline, self-control not adhering to precepts to regulate behavior. This is all done in *love* and in a *Spirit of Truth.* Counselors bring light by sharing helpful guidelines, safety rails, providing strategies to redirect and modify destructive behaviors to self and others. Counselors also have a mandate to encourage, comfort the fainthearted, uphold the weak, and demonstrate patience to all. Counseling is a judge free and safe space to be vulnerable, real, forthcoming and honest. To sit with a Counselor is to experience Jesus. Jesus shares in our humanity. Jesus actively listens and empathizes with patience. Jesus demonstrates grace, mercy, love, always giving helpful, supportive, truthful, and constructive feedback. Jesus empowers us to have faith encouraging perseverance and embracing hope despite difficult situations. Jesus challenges our thinking and helps us to reframe negative thinking.

Cognitive Behavioral Therapists are actually operating the way Jesus does. Cognitive Behavioral Therapy is an evidence-based psychological therapy that has scientific proven efficacy of helping people recover from mental health issues such as anxiety, depression, complicated grief, substance use disorders, trauma, anxiety disorders like social anxiety and panic disorders. CBT has also effectively treated obsessive -compulsive disorder, post-traumatic stress disorder, phobias, eating disorders, mood disorders such as bi-polar disorder, sleep problems, low-self-esteem, and issues like anger, chronic stress, and pain. The CBT practice model consists of focusing on thoughts and behaviors. CBT works by assisting individuals to identify distorted core beliefs about themselves that often contribute to negative thought patterns and behaviors that cause mental health challenges. CBT is a goal-oriented therapy and talk-therapy that helps individuals understand the connection between their thoughts, feelings, and behaviors.

Throughout my career I have often thrived as a Cognitive Behavioral Therapist gravitating more towards practicing CBT along with other psychological therapies. My experience and practice in the mental health field as a Qualified Mental Health Professional has allowed me to witness how this particular practice model has been very effective in helping others reconstruct their cognition, eliminate unhealthy thought patterns and behavioral patterns to improve their mental health. Jesus is the epitome of mental health. ***Philippians***

2:5 (NKJV) states, "Let this mind be in you which was also in Christ Jesus." So, if God tells us that we are to have the *mind of Christ* then, what does that mean? "The *mind of Christ* is the consummate mind of God. The mind of God is omniscient, supreme, and knows no insufficiency" (www.masters.edu, The Word Gives Us the Mind of Christ, 2025).

In order to know the mind of God you must make yourself available to sit with God and spend time with Him in order to begin thinking like Him. There are various ways to sit with God and spend time with Him. These ways include, sitting in silence, consciously opening your mind and spirit to hear from God, and to receive from God. Other ways consist of worshipping Him by singing to Him or basking in His presence as you listen to worship music. Praying, studying and meditating on the Bible, His Holy Word. These are just a few to mention as to how you can spend quality time with Him.

However, there is a protocol to hearing from God. God is a Holy God, and you can't just expect to hear from God or converse with Him if you are not willing to have a heart of repentance. You can't just demand to experience the fullness of God's presence when He is a Holy God, and you have full of uncleanness in your heart and life. In fact, God commands us to "be Holy for I am Holy" (1 Peter 1:16). Sin separates us from God. However, the love of God does not separate us from God. God loves us unconditionally yet while we were still found in sin. Love was given to us as the new law through Jesus. God sees us forgiven and made righteous through Jesus.

Therefore, we must come to God by the way of repentance. That means giving up our sinful nature asking for forgiveness. You must believe and accept Jesus as Lord and Savior. Allowing Jesus to have lordship over every aspect of your life. Jesus is the only way to God. We are to walk in a spirit of humility just as David exemplified in Psalms 51:10, when he prayed, "Lord, create within me a clean heart and renew a right spirit or steadfast spirit within me." God deemed David in the Bible as a man after God's own heart because David had a repenting heart, a heart of worship unto God esteeming God as sacred and Holy above everything else. Jeremiah, the prophet teaches us in the Bible as stated in ***Jeremiah 17:9 (KJV), "The heart is deceitful above all things, and desperately wicked: who can know it?"***

We often, here the cliché, to just *follow your heart* or *be led by your heart*. According to God, we are not to follow the heart because *the heart is deceitful*, it's flesh.

The heart is the soulish realm of where we harbor feelings. Feelings are fickle and change as quick as you can blink your eye. That's why God instructs us in Proverbs to *guard your hearts because out of the heart flows the issues of life.* Therefore, we must render our hearts and mind to God, and renew our minds daily with Word of God, the Holy Bible which is the *Sword of the Spirit* that pierces the carnal flesh. The carnality of our sinful nature that often leads us astray by the lust of the flesh are often contrary to the ways of Gods precepts in the Word of God. The Bible was written by man yet inspired by God's Spirit. So, we must honor the Word of God as being God's sacred manual of guidelines as to how we should think, behave, and live. The carnal, fleshly, sinful nature of us must die so we can live in the spirit and be led by the Spirit of God. You can't receive the spiritual things of God if you are not living in the Spirit and allowing the Holy Spirit to dwell within you as your teacher, comforter, guide in truth, disciplinary who convicts you in love when you are wrong and redirects you.

The issues of life can be trauma's that disrupted your life somewhere during your human developmental stages of life. Perhaps, the trauma hurt so badly that it opened your heart to offense, vindictiveness, unforgiveness, bitterness, jealousy, envy, strife, hostility, anger, shame, guilt, low self-worth, hatred, discord, fear, doubt, rejection, and so forth. You can't change what happened to you, but you can certainly change your perspective and choose to heal and recover from the trauma. Unprocessed crisis situations, disappointments, victimization, emotional and psychological pain, failures, shortcomings, loss, tragedies, and so forth can affect you in a horrific way. I have seen marriages destroyed. I have identified people's inability to have and maintain healthy relationships. I have also seen people unable to embrace the blessings in life because they're so paralyzed in hurt, offense, anger, and unforgiveness. However, you must examine your heart not allowing the issues of life to dictate your life, control your mind and emotions. God desires for you to live an abundant life despite the hardships.

Jesus tells us in John 16:33, *you will have trials and tribulations in this life but be of good cheer because I have overcome this world.* Jesus is helping us to take another approach to our thinking. It's only natural for us to think hopeless, powerless, revenge, defeat, etc. when we are faced with trials of life. However, when we open our spirit mind, our perspective changes, we see what Jesus is teaching us in the scripture passage, John 16:33, that what we face in this life is temporary. In other words, the distress that we experience now in this life is not comparable to what we will encounter when we move on from this life to eternal life in heaven where there will be no more pain, suffering, and tears. Jesus is teaching us that if this life is temporary, we should let go of the internal and external stressors that restricts us from receiving the joy that Jesus gives us despite of the tough obstacles we all face in this life on earth.

Psychologically speaking, the brain wires itself according to what thoughts and emotions we allow to entertain our minds and the soul (the heart). Your mind creates a landscape in the brain on the basis of lived experiences you have in life, your interactions, and how you emotionally and mentally responded. How you think matters. Your perception is your reality even if your reality is false. Your thoughts in relation to your negative experiences are worth paying attention to. What thoughts you choose to ponder on and let linger in your mind will become your thought patterns.

So, if the thoughts are toxic, non-productive, distorted with no evidence of being truth, and non-constructive they will now become your thought patterns established in your cognition as neural pathways. These pathways become your landscape in which your brain is now accustomed to as a normal way of thinking which may cause you to misconstrue information, have a misperception about people, situations, have false core beliefs, and cognitive distortions. These maladaptive thought patterns may lead to unhealthy behavioral patterns that may interfere with maintaining healthy relationships, emotional and mental stability, and lead to mental health disorders. Sometimes, these mental health disorders may need to be treated with medication to inhibit brain chemicals and hormones that are disrupted in production due to the malfunctioning of the brain wiring. This is why we are to be good stewards of our mind and thoughts. We are to steward well our mind, body, soul, and spirit.

Whole-person care is so vital. In such, if we neglect one of the whole person components of mind, body, soul, and spirit we are off balance. Mind, body, soul, and spirit are all interconnected. It is crucial that we monitor, keep account, and manage all four components so that we may prosper and be whole. The spirit is the core of who we are because we are spirit first. When God created humans, He breathed His Spirit in our physical bodies to give us life (Genesis 2:7). God's breath is the very essence of us being able to breath, live, and move. Our spirit is eternally linked to God. Our spirit brings everything in alignment to our physical being. When you nurture the spirit giving your spirit spiritual nourishment you are experiencing abundant life that only comes from God the *Creator of Life*.

The Spirit of God is your lifeline. Your spirit is what's connected to the lifeline. This is why it is extremely vital that you live in the spirit where there is life and peace. Rather than, live according to the carnal mind. Peace is given by God that surpasses your natural mental compacity or carnal mind to understand. God is the *peace giver* who calms the human mind from the rushing storming waves of thoughts. Often, those thoughts are intrusive that can be debilitating, cause disassociation, and cause you to go into flight stress response. Jesus is the *Prince of Peace*. ***Isaiah 26:3 (NKJV) states, "You will keep him in perfect peace, Whose mind is stayed on you, Because he trusts in You."***

God gives wisdom, knowledge, and counsel that overrides the law of physical matter such as your mind. Again, this is why God commands that you wash your minds with the Word of God what God has proclaimed and established as our guide to think like Him spiritually that is supernatural. In the book of Romans in chapter 8 of the Bible is a clear guide as to how we are to find life in the spirit that supersedes the human mind.

Romans 8:1-17 (NKJV) states, "There is therefore now no condemnation to those who are in Christ Jesus, who do not walk according to the flesh, but according to the Spirit. For the law of the Spirit of life in Christ Jesus has made me free from the law of sin and death. For what the law could not do in that it was weak through the flesh, God did by sending His own Son in the likeness of sinful flesh, on account of sin: He condemned sin in the flesh, that the righteous requirement of the law might be fulfilled in us who do not walk according to the flesh but according to the Spirit. For those who live according to the flesh set their minds on the things of the flesh, but those who live according to the Spirit, the things of the Spirit. For to be carnally minded is death, but to be spiritually minded is life and peace. Because the carnal mind is enmity against God; for it is not subject to the law of God, nor indeed can be. So then, those who are in the flesh cannot please God.

But you are not in the flesh but in the Spirit, if indeed the Spirit of God dwells in you. Now if anyone does not have the Spirit of Christ, he is not His. And if Christ is in you, the body is dead because of sin, but the Spirit is life because of righteousness. But if the Spirit of Him who raised Jesus from the dead dwells in you, He who raised Christ from the dead will also give life to your mortal bodies through His Spirit who dwells in you.

Therefore, brethren, we are debtors—not to the flesh, to live according to the flesh. For if you live

according to the flesh you will die; but if by the Spirit you put to death the deeds of the body, you will live. For as many as are led by the Spirit of God, these are sons of God. For you did not receive the spirit of bondage again to fear, but you received the Spirit of adoption by whom we cry out, "Abba, Father." The Spirit Himself bears witness with our spirit that we are children of God, and if children, then heirs—heirs of God and joint heirs with Christ, if indeed we suffer with Him, that we may also be glorified together."

The Mind of Christ is the way of thinking and having the perspective of Jesus Christ. To have the perspective of Jesus is to understand God's plan. The perspective of Jesus is accessible to believers through the Holy Spirit. To have *The Mind of Christ* is to share Jesus' compassion, prioritize humility and obedience. Essentially, as we receive *The Mind of Christ*, we begin to take on His nature and characteristics. You will begin to think and act like Jesus as to what He would do in any given situation. To have *The Mind of Christ* is to have access to Jesus' thoughts and purposes that in return enables a deeper understanding of God's Will. The key characteristics of Jesus is humility, compassion, prioritizing others first rather than yourself. *The Mind of Christ* is never to be self-absorbed only thinking about yourself. To have *The Mind of Christ* is to deny yourself and look at the bigger picture. We are to seek God's will above our personal desires and understand God's plan for salvation. God instructs us to not take on the ways of this world, ***"And do not be conformed to this world, but be***

transformed by the renewing of your mind, that you may prove what is that good and acceptable and perfect will of God." – Romans 12:2, NKJV.

Now, I am not at all saying we should not express our emotions, grieve, or experience random thoughts in association to the difficult and traumatic life issues that we all experience. We must certainly allow ourselves to be human and experience the real thoughts, emotions, and pain that comes with trials and tribulations. What I am saying is don't allow your human nature to dictate and control your life. Rather, let your spirit lead as the Holy Spirit leads when you lean into Jesus by taking His hand. Allow Jesus to walk with you through the storms of life. When you walk with Jesus allowing Him to be your *Wonderful Counselor,* He will make sure that the stormy waves of life will not overtake you. Jesus will show you how to look at negative situations from a different perspective. You will be able to see from a higher standpoint. Because, when you choose to walk with Jesus you are seated with Jesus in *heavenly places far above all principalities of evil and powers of darkness* (Ephesians 2:6) and see from heaven's viewpoint.

Believers who rely on Jesus to be their *Wonderful Counselor* while on earth carry a heavenly perspective into their daily lives. The benefits of walking hand and hand with Jesus is to experience triumph, honor, authority, protection from evil spirits and forces. Again, this thinking is supernatural. This type of thinking is *Kingdom-mindedness.* Kingdom-mindedness is opposite of how our natural mind functions. You see situations and this world as temporary and having no weight because you see God having supreme authority, dominion, and power over everything. In God you see that everything is working for the good and according to His purpose all for the advancement and preparation of His Kingdom. Kingdom-mindedness is eternal thinking. When you walk in this frame of thinking you are not moved by what you see in the physical world with the natural eye. Instead, you see things as they are in eternity. Eternal hope is what anchors the soul and stabilizes the mind as we are in our earthly bodies. ***"This hope we have as an anchor of the soul, both sure and steadfast, and which enters the Presence behind the veil, where the forerunner has entered for us, even Jesus, having become High Priest forever according to the order of Melchizedek." – Hebrews 6:19-20, NKJV.***

As 2 Corinthians 5:7 states, "For we walk by faith and not by sight" (NKJV). Therefore, we are not moved by the situations that we witness with the natural eye. Rather, we see things according to our faith in Jesus and looking at life situations with our spiritual eyes.

Therefore, as I mentioned earlier regarding Jesus and CBT, Jesus is the greatest Cognitive Behavioral Therapist that there ever was and is. In fact, He demonstrated this practice model first before it even became new knowledge to the scientific and psychological researchers. God is all knowledge and wisdom. Man received this knowledge and revelatory insight as God authorized them to discover it. The practice model of CBT is to combat negative thoughts, challenge negative thinking, replace thoughts with thoughts that are true and constructive, dispel false core beliefs that have been constructed over time in the human cognition. CBT involves positive self-talk to redirect thoughts that are non-productive, reframing thoughts with thoughts that are true, helpful, and constructive. Sounds a lot like Jesus! Jesus demonstrates how we are to take our *thoughts captive to make obedient to Christ.*

God challenges our thinking and commands us to use our spiritual authority that we have in Jesus. ***"Casting down arguments and every high thing that exalts itself against the knowledge of God, bringing every thought into captivity to the obedience of Christ." – 2 Corinthians 10:5, NKJV.***

The arguments in your mind that you have going back and forth in your mind or repeatedly that causes double mindedness is what God is commanding us to do in the above scripture passage, 2 Corinthians 10:5. God doesn't want us to be split in our thought process nor does He want us to have flighty, disorganized, and fragmented thinking. God tells us in scripture that a double-minded man is unstable in all of his ways (James 1:7-8). In the *American Psychiatric Association's Diagnostic And Statistical Manual of Mental Disorders, Fifth Edition, Text Revision* that healthcare providers, behavioral health providers, psychiatrists, psychologists, mental health counselors and other mental health professionals use when evaluating, assessing, diagnosing, and treating clients you will see that often prolonged fragmented thinking or disturbances in thought process is the basis for many mental health disorders. Prolonged mental instability changes the chemistry of the brain leading to mental illnesses. I often tell people that the brain is an organ like any other organ in the body. The brain can get ill and progressively decline even unto death. The neuroplasticity can be altered in a negative way where the neurons are no longer generating and building healthy networks in the brain causing the brain to remain idle with no electric activity firing off as the brain is wired to do so. The neurotransmitters are chemical messengers that carry signals between neurons and other cells in the body to help the various major body systems to function effectively. Neurotransmitters are essential for the body to operate appropriately and are involved in nearly every function of the body. They are critical for human behavior and cognition.

So, as you can see that not everything is a spiritual issue but either neurobiological or psychological. However, the physical body is connected to the spirit and often when we mismanage our physical body it opens the door for the spirit to malfunction because the *vain imaginations* (2 Corinthians 10:5) begin to take root blocking the mind to be open to receive *The Mind of Christ* that nourishes the spirit of man. Just as a person seeks treatment when the heart is not functioning as it ought to, causing cardiovascular issues or any other medical issues related to certain organs and body systems you must do the same for your mental health. Your mental health is part of the nervous system; central nervous system that involves the brain. The nervous system regulates complicated thought and memory processes essential as to how the body functions without thinking like blinking, sweating, and breathing.

The Word of God instructs believers to actively monitor and challenge thoughts that do not serve you or others well. God encourages us to challenge thoughts in the sense of making sure that they align with Gods truth which is exactly what CBT does in the restructuring process on the basis of truth when changing the cognition. Jesus encourages believers to transform their mind by consistently and habitually modifying their thinking by actively replacing negative thought patterns with positive thoughts which is a key element with CBT. Jesus, *The Wonderful Counselor (Isaiah 9:6),* guides and counsels people through personal struggles which aligns with the role of a therapist.

A therapist is an instrument in God's hand to chisel away at anything in the mind that doesn't belong. The cognitive coping strategies that a therapist engages clients to practice in life is a means to help people transform their minds. The holistic; whole-person care approach of a therapist which I often incorporate with Christ-centered, biblical, and psychological therapy is what helps a person become balanced in mind, body, soul, and spirit.

God is *The Great Physician* and *The Wonderful*

Counselor. The health of His creation, especially, His sons and daughters who have been adopted into the faith to be called the children of God through Jesus is extremely important to Him. To have overall good health is what God wants for His sons and daughters. If we are going to serve God, our physical body will need strength and the mental capacity to effectively carry the weight of His glory. We can be too spiritual that we are no earthly good. Otherwise, if all you focus on is the spiritual things and neglect the physical body and mental health you are not operating at optimal level. When there is a default in the mental health of a person, they will experience an imbalance. In such, they may experience distorted thinking that may disrupt the ability to accurately discern spiritually causing spiritual issues.

When a person lacks self-control or discipline as it relates to caring for the physical body there may be negligence of physical needs. For instance, a healthy diet, water consumption, regular exercise, adequate sleep, relaxation practices, time for physical touch, socialization, etc. are all key factors in caring for your physical and mental health. God expects us to be good stewards of our physical and mental health just as we care for our spiritual health. Physical and mental health are equally important as spiritual health. Physical health, spiritual health, and mental health are all systematically interconnected. These three parts of the human being needs to be balanced in every area in order to prosper as a whole person. God doesn't want us to be hindered with preventable physical and mental limitations that are debilitating. These debilitating physical and mental limitations are a result of prolonged repressed emotions, prolonged unprocessed psychological and emotional trauma that can lead to mood disorders, anxiety disorders, stress disorders, psychosomatic disorders to name a few.

Oftentimes, if a person does not manage internal and external stressors that may be associated with prolonged psychological distress, complicated unprocessed grief or unprocessed trauma the body keeps score. The brain and the body stores trauma. After a while the body can only store trauma or chronic stress for so long. Then, the body will begin to respond to the internal chronic stress. Physiological ailments will begin to manifest in all sorts of ways. Some of these physiological ailments could involve muscular-skeletal issues, joint pain, unexplained migraines, nervous system issues leading to anxiety, panic disorders, and cognitive impairment. Other physiological issues are gastrointestinal issues, ulcers, and gastroesophageal reflux disease. A weakened or compromised immune system is also a physiological issue that can lead to various infections such as frequent colds, flu, pneumonia, sinus infections, ear infections, skin infections, urinary tract infections, meningitis, bronchitis, and even more serious infections such as Fungai infections like esophageal candidiasis. Respiratory system issues, cardiovascular issues, diminished cells making you more prone to autoimmune diseases are among other physiological issues, and the list goes on.

If our physical and mental health are not good, then

it makes it very difficult to live out your life spiritually to carry out kingdom assignments for God in which you were called. As it says in the Bible in Matthew 26:41, *the spirit is willing, but the flesh is weak.* Jesus is telling us that we will have desires to do good but the flesh, the physical limitations of our human body interfere and lack strength. Now, I certainly know that there are simply medical issues that arise that are genetic, out of your control, and unpreventable. Perhaps, the illness or medical diagnosis is a result of a tragic event. However, what I am specifically talking about are illnesses and progression of illnesses that are brought on by prolonged chronic stress that could be treated medically and by psychological therapy.

As I indicated previously, our brains are like a computer. The brain needs to organize and process information. To give you a visual to help you understand and simplify how a healthy brain needs to function, the brain is like a file cabinet. The file cabinet helps store and organize information. The file cabinet has many hanging file folders that store pertinent information in labeled manilla file folders in an organized manner stored in a locked file cabinet that is secure. The person managing the stored and secured information in the file cabinet has the power and control to effectively keep track of how the information is stored and kept in a secure location. This is how your brain works.

You have the power and control to be a good steward of managing your brain. You are responsible for organizing your thoughts, life experiences, and feelings to ensure that it is being placed in a secure location of your brain so you can function effectively. You are responsible for nurturing brain health. You are responsible for processing information such as, trauma's, grief, emotional and mental distress to put into healthy perspective alleviating arrested development or stagnation and moving forward in life.

People get stuck in life mentally or emotionally due to issues that occurred in life and not processing what happened to get understanding, meaning, closure, inner peace, and healing. When this happens, people lose a sense of identity or develop a false identity. Trauma can disrupt the development of security, trust, healthy attachment during a crucial developmental stage in the human development. People may have felt powerless at some period in their life and can later on in life develop *personality disorders* (American Psychiatric Association Diagnostic and Statistical Manual of Mental Disorders, Fifth Edition, Text Revision). *Personality disorders* such as, *narcissistic personality disorder* or *borderline personality disorder* having problems with controlling, manipulating, and demising others (DSM-5- TR). Some people develop patterns of maladaptive behaviors such as co-dependency, power and control tactics which are toxic and abusive behaviors. Other maladaptive behaviors involve patterns of unhealthy relationships, substance abuse, addictive behaviors, self-harm behaviors, and compulsive behaviors. Some of these behaviors can develop symptoms of hypersensitivity, hypervigilance, hyperawareness, impulsivity, to name a few.

Counseling and psychotherapy are a means to maintain good mental health by organizing and processing what is recorded in the brain. Counseling and psychotherapy provide strategy, tools, and techniques that help support good mental health, enhancing cognition, restructuring cognition, promoting recovery, and the overall well-being of a person. Counseling assists people with developing healthy ways to nurture, care for, and balance mind body, soul, and spirit. You may have heard the cliché, *health is wealth.* Health most certainly is wealth! Your overall health is essential. You must make health a priority. You must value yourself to the point where you understand that you only receive one physical body to live in on this earth in this life. Therefore, you must steward well what God has given you and entrusted to you. God teaches us in His word that as much is given to us much is required of us. We are required by God to take care of our health that *we may prosper in all things and in health even as our soul prospers.*

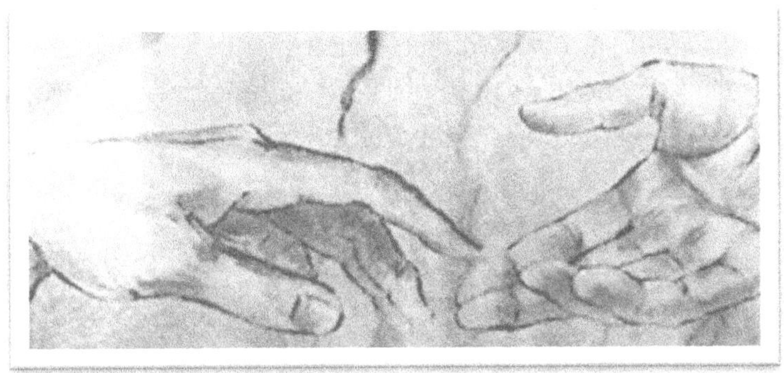

Chapter 3: The Prophetic Counselor

To be called to speak for God as His mouthpiece is an awesome mandate and privilege that only God Almighty can choose to anoint and ordain to fulfill His plan and purpose in the lives of others. You may ask, what is a *Prophetic Counselor*? In the Holy Bible, Ephesians 4:11 (NKJV) states, "***And He Himself gave some to be apostles, some prophets, some evangelists, and some pastors and teachers, for the equipping of the saints for the work of ministry, for edifying of the body of Christ, till we all come to the unity of the faith and of the knowledge of the Son of God, to a perfect man, to measure of the stature of the fullness of Christ.***"

The *Prophetic Counselor* is someone who has been chosen, anointed by the Spirit of God to know the mind of God, and to speak out what God is saying as His mouthpiece. The *Prophetic Counselor* carries *understanding* and *knowledge* which are two of the seven manifestations of the Spirit of God mentioned in Isaiah 11:2 which God has imparted into the person whom He has selected to operate at the capacity to equip and strengthen others who need edification.

Jeremiah 1:5 (NKJV) states, ***"Before I formed you in the womb I knew you; Before you were born I sanctified you; I ordained you a prophet to the nations."***

The *Prophetic Counselor* provides spiritual interpretation as the Spirit of God leads them in action of explaining or giving meaning to someone. Often, God will use the *Prophetic Counselor* to foretell or predict what is to come in a person's life by divine inspiration which is the gift of prophecy having the anointing on their life as a prophet to speak, *thus saith the Lord.* The *Prophetic Counselor* gives instruction and exhortation to communicate empathetically, under the divine unction of the Holy Spirit, urging someone to follow the wisdom and direction of God. God shows us in scripture to, ***"…Believe in the LORD your God, and you shall be established; believe His prophets, and you shall prosper." – 2 Chronicles 20:20, NKJV.***

It is always God, the Father's will that His people prosper. God desires His sons and daughters to obtain wisdom and understanding. Again, as mentioned in chapter 1, ***"Wisdom is the principle thing; Therefore,***

get wisdom. And in all your getting, get understanding." – Proverbs 4:7, NKJV.

Wisdom is the key, principle thing because wisdom is what helps us all navigate through this life. Godly wisdom is what gives you stability, directs you to make good decisions, and leads you to success in every aspect of your life. In order to obtain the wisdom of God we must first understand the importance of having a reverential fear, respect for God. Proverbs 1:7 (NKJV) states, ***"The fear of the LORD is the beginning of Knowledge, but fools despise wisdom and instruction."***

Proverbs 1:2-5 (NKJV) states, ***"To know wisdom and instruction, To perceive the words of understanding, To receive the instruction of wisdom. Justice, judgement, and equity; To give prudence to the simple, To the young man knowledge and discretion. A wise man will hear and increase in learning. And a man of understanding will attain wise counsel."***

The prophetic counseling anointing is a form of pastoral care to provide healing with prophetic revelatory insight. Many people are hurting emotionally, mentally, spiritually, and physically. People are wounded from various types of traumas and all sorts of chaotic issues. This is why the *Prophetic Counselor* is extremely instrumental to God in helping people heal and recover. The *spirit of counsel* and the *spirit of understanding* work in sync to help bring healing to the mind and soul of a person.

Often, the gift of healing will manifest during a

counseling session as the *Prophetic Counselor* is led by the Holy Spirit. The gift of discerning of spirits will also be on display due to God's ultimate purpose for truth to prevail and wholeness of an individual, couple, group or family. God will reveal to the *Prophetic Counselor* the driving forces, spiritual evil principalities that are at work, matters of the heart, hidden motives, underlying root issues, and intentions of a person contributing to the presenting problems. If the *Prophetic Counselor* is clinically trained, the counselor will use psychological tools such as specific assessments to identify patterns, behaviors, adverse childhood experiences to determine levels of trauma, trauma assessment, spiritual assessment, grief assessment, and assessing symptoms of mental health disorders or illnesses by doing a mental health assessment to determine a plan of care or treatment.

The *Prophetic Counselor* is compassionate and bear revelatory insight from God that allow the counselor to see through the lens of God into the hurts and wounds of people. Prophetic Counselors are invited into the world of the hurting and broken to walk with individuals in dark places with the goal in mind to lead them to a place of hope and healing. Prophetic counselors operate in the fruit of love, patience, gentleness, kindness, meekness, and self-control (Galatians 5:22). God entrusts the *Prophetic Counselor* with His people to handle them with His care. A counselor who is not skilled, lacking wisdom, knowledge, understanding, and does not operate in the fruits of the Holy Spirit especially, love can actually do more harm to a person in need rather than helping them.

Counseling is a calling and not everyone is called to this role. It is crucial that people who have a desire to be a counselor especially, a *Prophetic Counselor* to know that this is the mandate on their life. A person will be accountable unto God when operating in this ministerial role. Prophetic counselors are naturally gifted to listen well, empathize with others, and establish a healthy rapport with people allowing the person they are providing care for to feel safe and comfortable to become emotionally vulnerable. Establishing a good rapport helps individuals to be able to quiet their anguished soul and relieve their troubled hearts. When a person feels heard and understood then they feel valued. When a person feels valued then they feel respected and feel loved. Specific traumas has caused individuals to move on throughout life bleeding and with this persistent void of not feeling heard, understood, valued, respected, and loved. God being who He is, *The Good Shepherd* (John 10:11) knows the heart of all man. Therefore, He goes out to the hurting sheep who have been led astray, rejected, and abandoned to treat the wounds and bring them into the sheepfold. Jesus is more concerned about the one sheep that He leaves the 99 to go after the one who has strayed away from God (Matthew18:12).

Trauma:

Trauma and how the Prophetic Counselor responds to the traumatized:

Trauma is when an individual experiences very stressful, frightening, or distressing events that are too difficult to cope with, or it is out of the person's control. Leaving a person feeling powerless. These traumatic events are extreme or intense that can have a lasting negative impact on a person's life. Traumatic events can cause physical, emotional, and psychological stress and have lasting adverse effects on a person's overall well-being.

Traumatic events can include: a tragic sudden vehicle accident or any type of serious accidents, sexual violence; abuse, domestic violence, gun violence, school shootings, world health crisis/pandemic, humanitarian crisis, natural disasters, wars, terrorist attacks, physical injuries, terminal illnesses, sudden tragic loss/death of a loved one, miscarriage, loss of possessions or valuable assets, divorce, racism, discrimination, bullying, negligence, and abandonment, are some of the ideal traumatic events that occur in the lives of so many people across the world. Trauma can disrupt a person's sense of security or safety, identity; loss of self, cause emotional dysregulation, making it difficult to have healthy relationships with others. Shame, guilt, helplessness, hopelessness, powerlessness, or intense fear are some of the experiences people have in response to the trauma.

Traumatic reactions, trauma responses or symptoms may involve: Depression, anxiety, excessive worry, anger, socially withdrawn, hypervigilance, intrusive thoughts, nightmares, flashbacks, hypersensitivity, lack of interest in enjoyable activities, lack of motivation, lack of energy, negative thought patterns always thinking about the worst scenarios that could happen in any given situations. Everyone responds to trauma differently. The way people respond to trauma depends on; personality traits, resiliency, coping ability, world-views, current stressors, family dynamics, support systems, underlying medical issues, pre-existing mental health issues, past traumatic events, or what circumstances that person is already dealing with in their current stage of life.

The physiological effects of trauma involve: Fatigue, insomnia, digestive issues, stomach pain, migraines and headaches, racing heart, profuse sweating, jittery, and startle response. Other symptoms may involve nausea, vomiting, exhaustion, dizziness, visual changes, flashbacks, dissociation, and panic attacks. Trauma brings on chronic stress that may cause incapability to adapt to the sudden change or distress. Behavioral changes may be a result of inability to adapt or cope with the trauma. These behaviors manifest in maladaptive behaviors. Maladaptive behaviors include substance abuse such as tobacco use, nicotine use, smoking cigarettes and smoking more than usual. Other substances used, alcohol, illicit drugs, or abusing prescribed drugs such as opioids or narcotics. Maladaptive behaviors also include addictive behaviors, compulsive eating; eating too much, impulsive or erratic sexual behaviors that are destructive, sexual promiscuity that can develop into addictive behavioral patterns. Pornography, and gambling addiction are common maladaptive behaviors. These addictions may lead people to believe that this engagement is something that they can control temporarily alleviating the deeply embedded feeling of powerlessness associated with past trauma. A person can begin a pattern of neglecting physical health such as not maintaining a good diet, not exercising, and not keeping up with regular healthcare appointments. Poor hygiene or lack of grooming self nor caring about dress attire, appearing disheveled, and appearance is inappropriate are other self-negligent behaviors. Maladaptive behaviors are basically behaviors that people engage in that prevent them from effectively coping with situations or stressors in a healthy manner.

Trauma victims can get stuck and lack healthy coping skills that lead to unhealthy coping mechanisms such as patterns of avoidance or repressing emotions. Avoidance can lead to overwhelming internal stressors that contribute to self-harm behaviors, risky decision-making, which hinder a person's ability to adapt to their environment and can disrupt daily living and functioning. Maladaptive behaviors are non-constructive in managing life challenges or emotions. When an individual is experiencing maladaptive behaviors, it can sabotage relationships and the overall well-being of a person. People develop maladaptive behaviors as their personal way of managing stress, excessive worry, and anxiety even though it is an unhealthy strategy.

Passive-aggressive behavior and lashing out on others, always on defense mode, are also maladaptive behaviors that develop due to prolonged chronic stress or post-traumatic stress. Chronic stress is a long-term psychological or physiological response to stressors that persist over weeks, months, and even years. Chronic stress has significant negative impact on not only your mind but your entire body that can progress or worsen with time contributing to many serious illnesses. As you may have heard the old saying "stress can kill you." Well, that is definitely correct. Stress and post-traumatic stress can ultimately and literally kill you if you do not take care of yourself. Some of the serious illnesses that chronic stress can lead to are cardiovascular disease, heart disease, heart attacks, high blood pressure, and stroke.

Chronic stress can worsen a pre-existing medical issue of diabetes by raising glucose levels as a result of unhealthy behaviors. Obesity is a common illness associated with chronic stress leading to weight gain due to diminished gut health dysregulating the cortisol, the stress hormone making it very difficult to respond to stress resulting in having a poor human stress response system. Cancer has been linked to chronic stress due to prolonged stress can activate the body's inflammatory response which could contribute to the onset of some cancers. Stress can also suppress NK-cell activity which can weaken the immune system making you more susceptible to autoimmune diseases and other chronic diseases.

As a Trauma therapist, and in past mental health professional roles that I had throughout my 28-plus years of experience in the mental health field, I have seen how prolonged post-traumatic stress and chronic stress led to major maladaptive behaviors. I have identified how maladaptive behaviors are prevalent among trauma survivors. I have witnessed firsthand how unprocessed prolonged trauma can progress and develop into mental health disorders. I have seen how mental health disorders that are left untreated can progress neurobiologically manifesting into severe mental illnesses due to the change in the brain chemistry and nervous system. The brain can begin to deteriorate and become very ill. Just as I said previously, the brain being a vital organ can become ill overtime just as any other vital organ in the human body does.

So now that I provided some psychoeducation about trauma, the effects of trauma, prolonged chronic stress, post-traumatic stress, and maladaptive behaviors, I am going to show you how a *Prophetic Counselor* responds to a person who is suffering mentally, emotionally, physically, and even spiritually. As a *Prophetic Counselor*, I operate under the prophetic anointing and serve in the office of a Prophet. Although, I am skilled, trained, and educated, I have been given the *Spirit of Counsel* to rest on me for the purpose of building up, instilling hope, and providing healing. I am driven with the compassion of Jesus to sit with the broken-hearted and to bind up the wounds (Psalms 147:3). To engage with those who are grieving, sharing in their grief as Jesus, the *Man of Sorrows* (Isaiah 53:3) bears grief and understands grief. Jesus, God manifested in the flesh left heaven to become human to experience the same suffering of humanity.

Jesus experienced and endured times of sadness. Jesus wanted to share in our humanity. Jesus even experienced extreme anxiety, stress, and fear to the point he was sweating drops of blood referred to hemato-hidrosis, a rare phenomenon in response to extreme levels of stress and fear. The bloody sweat was a physical manifestation of the intense internal struggle that Jesus was experiencing. This was a neurobiological and physiological response to chronic stress. Jesus was having a human experience. His physical body was responding to the internal stress and fear that we too as humans face when a real-life struggle is too heavy for the human body to handle. Stress, fear, anxiety, grief as it relates to being betrayed by Judas, denied by Peter, the rejection, abandonment, and hatred of His own people were all the human emotional reactions that Jesus was experiencing while praying in the Garden of Gethsemane. Jesus knew that the time had come where He was going to face His death, the crucifixion which brought on psychological and emotional distress contributing to a physiological response. What Jesus was experiencing was not a lack of faith nor was it a spiritual weakness. This was the SON OF GOD, JESUS being emotional vulnerable as a human being! Jesus was providing validation to all of us that it is certainly okay to express emotional vulnerabilities rather than avoiding our emotions. Jesus even cried out in great agony to the Father, ***"Father, if you are willing, please take this cup***

from me; yet not my will, but yours be done." – Luke 22:42, NIV.

Jesus, like some of us had to do, accepted the suffering yet ultimately submitted to God's Will in spite of the suffering.

The Holy scriptures teach us that as much is given much is required. Luke 12:48 (NKJV) states, ***"…For everyone to whom much given, from him much will be required…"*** I have been given a great and awesome responsibility and mandate to serve as a *Prophetic Counselor*. However, with that being said, I also had to count the cost and be willing to walk through seasons of personal crushing and suffering that caused me to develop spiritually, die to my flesh, grow in wisdom, and obtain an increase of compassion to help others. Most importantly, a pure oil of God's anointing came from the crushing and suffering that I endured. Just as pure olive oil comes from the crushing of olives, so it is with the *oil of gladness* referenced to the Holy Spirit and Jesus. In the crushing, Jesus becomes tangible, and His Spirit exudes out of us. My personal crushing that God authorized as I endured trials and tribulations allowed me to share in the suffering of Jesus. Therefore, I too might share in His glory. His glory is seeing the salvation of many! God is my Deliverer, Jehovah Mephalti! He is my healer, Jehovah Rapha!

I have witnessed many lives beyond count who were blessed by the oil of God's anointing that came out of my own crushing, and suffering. As Jesus tells us that we must be willing to lay down our life, deny ourselves-our hurt, offense, negative emotions, etc. and pick up our cross to follow Jesus (Matthew 16:24). That means I had to be willing to walk through some great hardship and not take it personal but count it all joy as James says in the Bible in James 1:2-3 (NKJV), ***"...count it all joy when you fall into various trials, knowing that the testing of your faith produces patience."***

Patience and perseverance developed in me when I walked through various adverse childhood experiences throughout my developmental stages of life before the age of 18, crisis situations throughout my adulthood, and at the age of 41 in 2018 when I experienced an unimaginable tragedy of losing my only son in a car accident who was 20 years old. I had to endure traumatic grief and post-traumatic stress. What I experienced wasn't meant to destroy me. Instead, it developed me and brought me to a spiritual maturity that will open heaven to others and experience God through me and my walk with Jesus. Moreover, that I may be considered worthy as a vessel of honor ready to serve as Jesus' true disciple (2 Timothy 2:21).

The Bible tells us in Isaiah 10:27, that *it is the anointing that destroys the yoke*. The anointing is God's power to remove burdens and to destroy the yoke. Figuratively speaking, the yoke is what ties or binds up a person, entangles, and tries to suffocate the life out of a person. The yoke is paralyzing, oppresses, and prevents a person from moving forward in life. The anointing is what delivers God's sons and daughters and sets the captives free. Prolonged trauma, grief, crisis situations, chronic stress, and mental health disorders is what holds so many people captive in their minds, emotions, physical bodies, and hinders the spirit to flourish and live as it was intended to on earth as it is in heaven. When God anoints someone with His power, it is literally God resting on flesh and does what the human flesh can't do. It's God's supernatural power that does the impossible!

So, as a *Prophetic Counselor* I respond to the traumatized, grief stricken, and mentally distressed with compassion, empathy, validation, emotional and psychological support. I provide each individual who I serve when providing counseling and psychotherapy services, a sense of safety, trust, and security which are the three most essential elements for creating reliability, stability, protection, confidence, and free from harm. When a person experiences sudden tragedy, traumatic events, crisis situations, and loss, life becomes uncertain and usually these essential elements that I mentioned go out the window. My role as God's instrument or tool in His hands is to allow the process of building a healthy rapport with the person who I am helping. I once had a clinical supervisor, Dr. Brenda Gilbert, licensed psychologist who wrote the foreword of this book, tell me many years ago, that I had a natural God-given ability to build a rapport with people immediately at the initial counseling and therapy session. I never forgot about that. It serves today as a reminder that every person God appoints to me to help, I can rest assure they will feel accepted, respected, valued, loved, feel safe, and able to trust the healing God in me right away. Establishing a healthy professional therapeutic rapport is vital to the counseling process. If a client does not feel comfortable or safe, they will not be willing to open up and expose their emotional vulnerabilities.

I recall even just the day before I was writing this chapter, when I was conducting a psychotherapy and counseling session at my private practice, with a client, who had suffered an astronomical amount of horrendous traumatic events in her life, indicated to me, *I don't know why I feel so comfortable to share parts of my life with you what I have never been able to open up about to anybody.*

My response to her was, "It's because you feel safe and comfortable due to feeling heard, understood, and valued." This client is 61 years old and the majority of what has happened to her happened so many years ago. However, the years of repressed emotions, patterns of avoidance, suppressed feelings, prolonged unprocessed complex trauma and post-traumatic stress has led her to develop years of maladaptive behaviors. These maladaptive behaviors include the loss of identity due to trauma disrupting development of a healthy identity. The disrupted self-identity led her into abusive relationships. As well as being randomly sexually victimized in a single violent sexual assault by a man who was on a search list for murdering someone. These traumas then led her to alcohol abuse; addictions and alcoholism to the point she almost lost her life due to the extreme levels of toxicity in her blood and poor organ functioning caused by the alcohol. She finally reached breaking point and made a conscientious decision to check herself into an intensive inpatient drug and alcohol recovery facility. Now, here she is with me in my care 53 days of sobriety as God divinely ordered her steps to meet me. I recall telling her that, "It's your time to heal!"

You see, when God has established a place of healing you can guaranteed that He will make sure that the hurting, broken, and sick will come and receive divine healing that only comes from Him. I often say, I get a front row seat to watch the miraculous take place in my counseling office that I have declared as "God's Healing Room." I am just a conduit for His Spirit to operate through. I have seen this woman twice now and I can already see the divine healing taking place. Usually, counseling, and long-term psychotherapy is a process that takes time to unravel the years of intertwined mess of various detrimental life experiences that has entangled a person. Henceforth, oftentimes as an onion, there are layers of trauma, hurt, and extreme difficult life situations that have occurred in a person's life. Overtime, those layers of trauma has enclosed a person's core identity of who they truly are. Those layers have to be pulled back one layer at a time to get to the core of that person so that person can reclaim their life and identity.

God is the God of restorative health! God has a way of meeting you in the valley. I recall an old hymn; "The Blood Will Never Lose Its Power" (Civilla D. Martin, 1866-1948, and Walter Stillman Martin (1862-1912);

Thurston Frazier, 1962, 1966- "It Will Never Lose Its Power", Andre Crouch, FRAZIER-CLEVLAND CO.). The hymn emphasized how Jesus' blood that was shed on Calvary gives us strength daily and reaches everyone of all socio-economic, racial, and cultural status. The blood of Jesus reaches those in high places and those in low places, and who are experiencing a valley season. The blood of Jesus is so powerful that it will never lose its power.

I am a living testament of this power found in Jesus and what He has done for each one of us on the *Cross of Calvary* to find eternal hope and healing. This client's story that I have shared is one of countless stories that I was given the privilege to see the *Author and Finisher* of our faith, God Himself, restore the mental health and overall health for so many who God used me to reach by His Spirit, anointing, and power. Strategy is what it takes as a *Prophetic Counselor* to lead people out of darkness and despair. As I mentioned before, God is Truth so as a *Prophetic Counselor*, I too must operate in truth and allow the Holy Spirit to lead others into truth. As we all have heard many times, that "truth will set you free." Well, just as the Word of God says, that where the Spirit of the Lord is there is freedom (2 Corinthians 3:17). Often, prolonged trauma can create cognitive distortions such as: *overgeneralizing, jumping to conclusions, emotional reasoning, personalization, labeling, catas-trophizing, mind reading, blaming, magnification and minimization, mental filtering, discounting positives, and selective abstraction*, Beck, J.S. (2021), Beck et al.,

(1979), Burns, (1980). I will discuss cognitive distortions in more detail later in the book. These patterns of unhealthy thinking patterns can become someone's reality due to having these distortions as a normal way of thinking becoming a person's perception that eventually becomes reality to them. This is how mental disorders develop which create unhealthy behavioral patterns. False core beliefs are also something that trauma survivors establish overtime due to the patterns of distorted thoughts.

The *Prophetic Counselor* is accountable unto God to speak truth to dismantle deception, lies; that which is not true, help people to identify false core beliefs, and identify irrational thought patterns to eliminate poor choices that lead to maladaptive behavioral patterns that could be self -destructive. Cognitive Processing Therapy is a way to help clients process thoughts and lived traumatic experiences to allow clients to talk about what they haven't been able to discuss with anyone. Cognitive processing helps people alleviate the emotional and psychological weight of the various traumas. Giving people the opportunity to get everything up and out telling their life story is what releases the heavy burden and brings healing. In fact, Jesus tells us that we are more than overcomers by the blood of the lamb, who is Jesus and the word of our testimony which is what you have endured (Revelation 12:11). Jesus tells us to *come to Me all who are heavy laden, and I will give you rest, for My yoke is light* (Matthew 11:28). My role is to gently, and patiently facilitate open communication, expression of feelings, to allow space and time for clients to express feelings, organize thoughts, process experiences, actively listen, provide empathy, and validation. Often, what happens during this process when a person is hearing what they are saying out loud, helps them to make sense of everything they endured and put experiences into healthy perspective.

I then ask pertinent questions when assessing trauma or mental health history, and point out underlying root causes of thoughts, and behavior. Then, I give positive feedback, engage client in self-awareness, and empower client to identify ways that they can improve. Counseling opens the door to teach, advise, encourage, comfort, confront, challenge, correct, and assist with developing new healthy and constructive coping strategies. Constructive coping strategies alleviate problematic issues and eliminate symptoms of mental health issues. Collaborative approach is a strategy used in the counseling process to engage client in the problem-solving process with the counselor to develop solutions. As I am collaboratively working with the client, we are working together as a team effort to define client goals and explore problematic issues. The counselor and the client are partnering in mutual agreement to obtain resolution, healing, and recovery. This collaborative strategy gives clients an opportunity to become aware of their capabilities of obtaining healing and improving themselves by simply putting some effort into their recovery.

The strength-based therapeutic approach is also a

counseling strategy that helps people in counseling to identify their strengths and engages the client to get into the habit of practicing utilizing those strengths. The client learns how to apply those strengths in their healing and recovery journey. As you can see, the *Prophetic Counselor* is operating as Jesus operated in the Bible, He always challenged people's thoughts, and empowered them to believe, to have hope, faith, and to identify that their strength comes from God. The Holistic therapeutic approach is another counseling strategy that helps people to understand the interconnectedness of mind, body, soul, and spirit. Whole-person care is the model for holistic psychotherapy. Encouraging people to develop good self-care practices that include mental health care such as relaxation, mindfulness; practicing grounding yourself in the present moment engaging your senses to enjoy the here and now alleviating anxiety, worry, stress, fear, etc. as well as physical care, and spiritual care.

Developing an exercise regimen promotes good physical health as well as mental health by regulating brain chemistry. Exercise is good practice for mental health. When you exercise, you are increasing heart rate, promoting blood flow that carries oxygen to the brain which regulate production of brain chemicals such as serotonins, endorphins, dopamine's, oxytocin, GABA (Gamma-aminobutyric acid), etc. These major brain chemicals promote motivation, regulate mood, enhances sleep, appetite, social interaction, enhances trust, and bonding, feelings of well-being, and reduces anxiety. Exercise helps your brain feel happy, pleasurable, calm, and you experience cognitive enhancement to think sharper and faster. The brain fires effectively and establishes healthy neural networks when you exercise.

Healthy diet, sleep, water consumption, preventative healthcare appointments, and maintaining routine wellness check-ups are also extremely important for promoting physical health. As mentioned earlier, brain health results in good mental health. Allowing yourself to openly express feelings, understand your feelings by paying attention to what you are feeling, and give validity to your feelings are all good soul care practices. Spiritual care is also emphasized when providing whole-person care when using the holistic approach. As a *Prophetic Counselor*, Christ-centered, Biblical, and spiritual counseling is the primary focus of the counseling process.

The goal is to connect individuals to God and encourage them to invite God into their situation and their life. I help clients understand the importance of using their imagination and seeing it as a gift from God that is a key to open heaven and seeing their situation from God's perspective. Inspiring clients to imagine God in the counseling room with them every time they attend a counseling session and outside of the counseling session is the goal of the *Prophetic Counselor*. This spiritual technique empowers people to have faith that unlocks the door to see what they once saw as impossibilities as now possibilities. I love what Jesus says in Matthew 19:26 (NIV), ***"Jesus looked at them and said, With man this is impossible, but with God all***

things are possible."

The *Prophetic Counselor* helps individuals see how God views their situation and as the Holy Spirit leads, the *Prophetic Counselor* speaks on behalf of God to bring a new perspective, and to change the trajectory of the individual's thoughts, behavior, perception, patterns, and course of life. Spiritual health is the lifeline of the whole-person care model. Therefore, when assisting a person to care for and balance mind, body, soul, and spirit, there is a great emphasis on leading others to strengthen their relationship with Jesus. The *Prophetic Counselor* encourages prayer, meditation, worship, reading and studying biblical scripture, connecting with a community of faith; a spirit-filled and full gospel Bible teaching believing church during counseling sessions. The focus is to help individuals to apply the biblical scriptures to daily living and be a doer of the Word of God rather than just a hearer (James 1:22) of the Word of God.

The *Word of Wisdom* is one of the primary gifts in operation during counseling sessions which entail the supernatural impartation of factual things that are occurring in the life of the individual as well as to give guidance, and solutions. The spiritual gifts are interactively working together in unity with revelatory gifts such as *Word of Knowledge,* the supernatural insight or understanding given by God to enlighten an individual, and the *gift of discernment*. The gift of discernment is pertinent to the function of the *Prophetic Counselor* in such, having understanding, perceiving the true nature of a person, understanding the source and meaning of spiritual events. The *Prophetic Counselor* will be able to discern whether or not there is demonic spiritual influence or a heavenly spirit in a person's life. Exposing lies and lying spirits are discerned in counseling sessions as the Lord reveals to the counselor to protect individuals and to establish truth. God exposes darkness to keep believers from being led astray.

The *Prophetic Counselor* helps others to take action towards what is spiritually and mentally profitable, that which is good and godly. Discernment is a responsibility of the *Prophetic Counselor* to manage with gentle care, kindness, and love when pointing out spiritual error in order to improve mental health and behaviors of a person. These spiritual and revelatory gifts are usually in full operation in the counseling process to provide supernatural solutions to troublesome situations and dilemmas presented in counseling. The *Prophetic Counselor* will pray with their clients, speak over the situation during the counseling session inspired by the Holy Spirit, and operate in the gifts of the Holy Spirit previously mentioned. The goal is to help people experience the healing and resurrecting power of God through the sensitive compassionate ministry of a *Prophetic Counselor*.

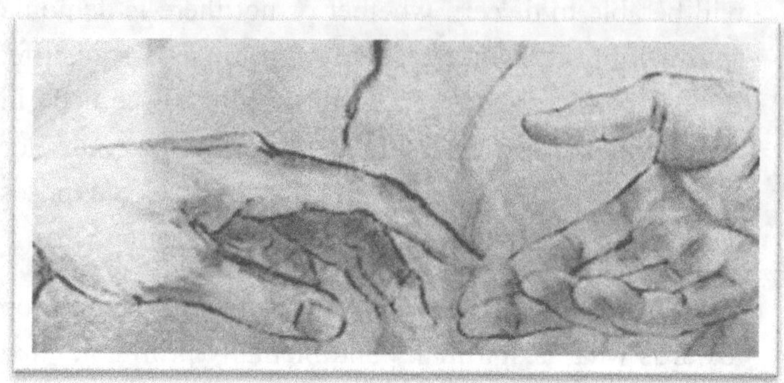

Chapter 4: The Great Physician

"He sent His word and healed them, And delivered them from their destructions" Psalms 107:20, NKJV.

Jesus Christ was given the title in the Bible and the early church referred Jesus as the "Divine Physician." Jesus says, ***"Those who are well have no need of a physician, but those who are sick. I have not come to call the righteous, but sinners, to repentance." – Luke 5:31-32, NKJV.*** Jesus is expressing in this scripture passage how the need for a physician and what the physician's practice of medicine is necessary for those who are *sick*. Spiritual healing and healing for the soul comes when a sinner comes to Jesus, repents of sin, and receives Jesus as Lord and Savior. Yielding to God in obedience, and God transforming you by allowing the Word of God to become the *Living Word* in your life is how spiritual healing is manifested.

However, sometimes physical healing doesn't always come in the form of an instantaneously, supernatural, and miraculous way. There are times when physical healing in the body whether physically or mentally comes in the form of utilizing medicine that was innovatively created by men who were given wisdom and knowledge by God to formulate as a means of healing. Proverbs 2:6 teaches us that ALL wisdom and understanding comes from the Lord. The Lord is the epitome of knowledge and understanding. He is "ALL WISDOM!" God provides men and women with knowledge, creative skills, and experiences to establish physical healing. So, as we are spiritual beings, we are also physical beings that have physical needs in order to function at optimal health in both our body and mind.

We can't just solely expect God to miraculously heal and restore our physical health through prayer and avoid being proactive in promoting good physical health. We cannot violate the natural laws to maintain good physical health. For instance, you cannot expect God to miraculously heal you of sugar diabetes yet continue to eat unhealthy foods, do not exercise, and drink unhealthy beverages with high sugary content rather than water or other healthy beverages. I have seen when God miraculously healed a person of a disease or serious illness and that person failed to do their part in maintaining good diet and exercise on a consistent basis and that illness returned. In the same way, you can't expect God to restore your mental health by just simply praying but not doing your part to go to counseling to process trauma, grief, crisis situations, and learn healthy cognitive coping strategies. As well as for others to learn how to break unhealthy toxic thought and behavioral patterns that contribute to mental disorders and mental illnesses. You have to do your trauma, grief, and mental health work to maintain a good healthy mind.

For some people, due to prolonged chronic stress, post-traumatic stress, depression, anxiety, addictive behaviors-addictions etc., the body has progressively developed neurobiological and psychological issues. These issues require medication to regulate and stabilize the brain chemistry, and specific body systems that were dysregulated due to internal stressors. These internal stressors associated with prolonged unprocessed traumatic or stressful events that have occurred in your life can contribute to neurobiological and psychological issues. I often share with clients when providing psychotherapy, that the physical human body and brain can only retain emotional trauma, psychological trauma, repressed emotions, and suppressed feelings contributing to internal stress for so long and then the body will eventually respond. The responses can be detrimental.

Excessive worry can progress into debilitating anxiety. Fear can progress into paranoia. Deep sorrow, despair, and complicated grief can progress into major depressive disorder. Distorted thinking or beliefs can lead to delusion, dissociation, and detachment from reality. Medication is very necessary to stabilize but it is not a cure all. Medication serves as an aid to promote mental health but is not meant to be dependent on it. You must do the work as well to maintain good mental health and obtain counseling/psychotherapy.

I think about the scripture passages when Jesus heals a blind man on two different occasions once with mud that He created by spitting on the dirt to make mud, a natural element of the earth which are the basic substances found on earth and in nature (John 9:6-25). In Mark 8, Jesus spit on the eyes of a blind man. In Mark 8:22-26, Jesus uses his own spit, saliva again as a natural substance. Organic matter was used to heal a man who was medically blind, an illness of the eyes. The common elements of organic matter are silicon, oxygen, aluminum, calcium, sodium, magnesium, and iron. The foundational elements of organic matter are carbon, hydrogen, oxygen, and nitrogen.

Mud primarily contains minerals that God created in the earth a mixture of quartz, clay minerals-kaolinite, illite, montmorillonite, feldspar, carbonates, calcite, dolomite. Human saliva consists of 99.5 % water, the 5% consist of electrolytes, including sodium, potassium, calcium, magnesium, bicarbonate, lipids, and phosphates. These are often some common elements and ingredient compounds found in today's medicine to treat various illnesses. Electrolytes are chemicals that conduct electricity when dissolved in water. Electrolytes assist with regulating nerve and muscle function and rebuilds damaged tissue. The oculomotor nerve is a vital nerve that carries commands from your brain to muscles for vital eye function. Also, found in human saliva are immunoglobulins, proteins/peptides, enzymes, mucins, chloride, and nitrogenous products. I don't want to get too deep into the science of medicine because I am not a medical doctor. However, I want to prove a point here as to what Jesus was demonstrating. That it is certainly okay to use science in treating physical and mental illnesses.

However, I do feel it is very necessary to give you some medical science background to help you understand the importance of science that was, is, and will always be what God has provided to man on earth to do even *greater works* that Jesus prophesied that we would do to perform healing and miracles. ***"Most assuredly, I say to you, he who believes in Me, the works that I do will do also; and greater works than these he will do, because I go to My Father." – John 14:12, NKJV.***

Even Jesus demonstrated to us during His ministry on earth the importance of science that can bring healing. Jesus emphasized in the previous mentioned scriptures that He brings both spiritual healing for the soul through repentance of sin as well as brings physical healing by the use of natural scientific elements found in the earth. When God created man, we were created from the dirt/dust of the earth and in that same earthly substance we can find so many life-giving, healing components, and healing properties. I hope you can see that not everything is spiritual but physical too that need medical attention and not just spiritual attention alone. Yes, we always utilize the power of prayer to activate the gift of faith, healing, and miracles. Yet, God does not exclude science and medicine to help bring divine healing to the sick. We are to speak the Word of God in faith to proclaim physical healing just as what God has declared to us in that, He sent forth His Word to heal in conjunction to obtaining medical care too.

Now, let's take a closer look at mental illnesses. Mental illness is when a wide range of specific conditions affect mood, thinking, and behavior. The Bible highlights the connection of mental health and spiritual health. This world is imperfect. We will all experience distress in this life. Whether it's loss, violence, grief, terminal illness, abuse, family dys-function, rejection, abandonment, hatred, divorce, natural disasters, a vehicle accident, major physical injuries, and the list goes on and on. Psalms 34:17-18 depicts how humans will be *crushed* and be *broken-hearted.* We will all experience crying out for help in desperation as a result of distress and trouble. In this life there will be perplexity, hardships, and complex circumstances.

Mental illness is not a reflection of a person's actions nor is a person defined by their mental illness. Mental illness is not a person's reflection of their lack of faith or spirituality. Mental illness is a reminder to all of us that we live in a world that is imperfect, uncertain, and unpredictable. Life can throw some serious blows. Often, these life blows are unanticipated. We don't expect bad things to happen. Yet, they do every day. It is crucial that we understand that this life is fragile and temporary. This life is like a vapor. You will not know what will happen tomorrow. A vapor is like a fog, puff of smoke, or a wisp that you see coming from steam, and then it eventually disappears.

"***Whereas you do not know what will happen tomorrow. For what is your life? It is even a vapor that appears for a little time and then vanishes away." – James 4:14, NKJV.*** We have to live this life with an eternal mindset. Mental illness is often a result of not seeing things eternally rather being moved or shaken by what we see or experience in the natural with the physical eye. Then, mental illness simply occurs just because this world is fallible. People often see this life as being forever. You can become complacent in this life thinking that this is all that there is. When in fact, this physical world and life is not at all the finality of our existence. I love what my Pastor said at my son's funeral in 2018. He stated, "The reason why death seems so abnormal to us because we were not created for death we were created for eternity." So many times, a state of shock hits us when faced with devastation, destruction, loss, and death. It's like our breath is taken from us in the moment when we experience trouble.

When we take our focus off of eternity and the God who holds us and everything together, who rules this world and reigns in supreme power in Heaven and on earth we lose peace and soundness of mind. Of course, in our human nature we are allowed to feel the shock, devastation, and feelings as a result of the trial and tribulation that we experience. However, we must allow God to assist us. God is our present help in the time of trouble. ***"God is our refuge and strength, A very present help in trouble." – Psalms 46:1, NKJV.***

God doesn't expect us to become reclusive, withdrawn, emotionally and mentally shut down, suppressing or repressing our feelings, and become stagnant in life. Better yet, He wants us to persevere, grow, and develop spiritual strength as we face trials and tribulations. God is our Savior; He saves us and delivers us. All we have to do is call on Him, trust Him, and simply believe in Him to bring us out mentally, spiritually, emotionally, and physically.

"The righteous cry out, and the Lord hears, And delivers them out of all their troubles. The Lord is near to those who have a broken heart, And saves such as have a contrite spirit. Many are the afflictions of the righteous, but the Lord delivers him out of them all," – Psalms 34:17-19, NKJV.

To be afflicted means to be struck with a problem, trouble, suffering, pain, and opposition. ***"We are hard-pressed on every side, yet not crushed; we are perplexed, but not in despair, persecuted, but not abandoned; struck down, but not destroyed." – 2 Corinthians 4:8-9, NKJV.***

Furthermore, ***"We always carry around in our body the death of Jesus, so that the life of Jesus may also be revealed in our body." – 2 Corinthians 4:10, NIV.*** In

Christ, we will experience the suffering as Jesus did. We will hurt. At times, we'll feel beat down, feel sorrowful, abandoned, rejected, and forsaken. However, we also experience the resurrecting power of Jesus giving us life in the midst of our suffering, when we come out of our season of tribulation, and when we enter eternity, Heaven.

This world being a falling world and is corruptible we will all experience afflictions and we will *feel crushed,* but the truth of the matter is, feelings are temporal and fickle they are subject to change. The resounding truth according to 2 Corinthians 4:8-9 tells us, we are "not crushed." We just feel like we're crushed. Feeling crushed is a real and valid feeling. However, as I mentioned, *feelings are subject to change*. There are times when we experience life curves that thrust us into a state of feeling confused, puzzled, worried, because you simply do not understand. You will feel like life has just paused for you as a result of trouble. You will feel like you can't take another move in life. You'll feel like the world is caving in on you. You will have feelings of despair when struck down with life difficulties leaving you feeling all alone, and even abandoned. Opposition will come. You will experience persecution or ill-treatment in this life. However, God has proclaimed to us all in His word, *we are perplexed, but not in despair, we are not abandoned* nor are we *destroyed* even though we may feel like it. Again, these feelings are real and valid. Yet, we must remember that God does not abandon us, nor are we destroyed to the point where we can't get back up again and keep persevering through life's journey.

Biblical Counseling can create a space for people with mental distress, mental illnesses, or disorders to share their lived experiences, understand the human condition, and their connection to God. The Bible gives profound examples and accounts of people who struggled with mental health. Mental health struggles are real. This life presents many struggles, and the struggle is real! We shouldn't be ashamed or embarrassed of experiencing real life struggles. We are humans and imperfect living in an imperfect world. The Bible provides spiritual coping mechanisms and gives meaning for mental health challenges. We are created to interact with other humans. Therefore, we have to put away the stigma of mental health counseling. As people of the Christian Faith, we can't frown upon mental health issues and see mental health issues as a spiritual deficiency.

Mental health issues are a human response to life difficulties. In fact, we have a human stress response system that is neuro-physio-biologically and psychologically systematic when faced with stressful situations. God knew that as humans we were going to experience stress in this life. We have a fight, flight, and freeze response that involves the autonomic and sympathetic nervous system preparing the human body to respond to perceived danger. It is the human body's natural response to stress. The brain detects perceived threat activating the amygdala to process emotions sending signals to the hypothalamus. The hypothalamus activates the sympathetic nervous system to release hormones like adrenaline and cortisol. These stress hormones trigger a cascade of physiological changes. These physiological changes increase heart rate, breathing, dilate pupils, increase blood flow to muscles, and heightened alertness. These prepare your body to go into an action of fight; aggression or confrontation in defending yourself, fleeing; running away or detaching your mind and emotions from reality, or freezing; avoiding the danger physically, mentally, or emotionally. This is the survival mechanism of humans.

We were created to feel, express pain, and heartache. Sometimes, people do not know how to do that. Perhaps, people grew up in an era, culture or family system that defined emotional vulnerability as a sign of weakness, lack of faith, or not necessary to talk about. This distorted core belief caused many to repress; prohibit emotional expression, suppress thoughts, feelings, or desires in response to a traumatic event, crisis situation, or hardship. Many haven't had the opportunity to be validated, empathized with, or taught that what happened to them was not their fault and out of their control. Perhaps, this is what you have experienced?

Now, without focusing so much on all the various categories of mental disorders such as, mood disorders, stress disorders, anxiety disorders, addictive disorders, and psychotic disorders to name a few of many, I will zero in for a moment on one category and generally discuss. I would like to focus a little on one category of the plethora of mental disorders that is very common. I don't want to get too focused in on clinical diagnoses. I believe that God is wanting to remove the labels off of people and bring true healing to the minds and psyche of many people.

As a Psychotherapist, I have seen that, today in society, many people who have suffered from powerlessness, associated with some form of trauma or hardship, at some point throughout their human lifespan development, struggle with deeply embedded insecurities. People then mask the repressed or suppressed feeling of powerlessness with exemplifying having power and control to feel secure within themselves even if it's abusive to others. As a result, many have developed *personality disorders* (American Psychiatric Association, 2022). A *personality disorder* involves a progressive, developed, long-term, inflexible, and unhealthy pattern of thinking and behaviors. People with *personality disorders* experience emotional instability that include extreme mood swings, intense instability to maintain relationships, manipulation, or have impulsive behaviors. Such as, lashing out on others, implying power and control, paranoid thoughts, suspicion or believing something to be real but is not reality. Some people with *personality disorders* may exemplify having special powers or seeing themselves as superior over others. *(American Psychiatric Association's Diagnostic and Statistical Manual of Mental Disorders, Fifth Edition, Text Revision), (With Emphasis).*

There are 10 specific types of personality disorders that are very common:

1. **Antisocial Personality Disorder:** Pervasive pattern of disregarding the rights of others, manipulative, deceitful, and have impulsive behaviors.

2. **Avoidant Personality Disorder:** Social inhibition out of fear of rejection or criticism; anxious, feelings of inadequacy, and hypersensitivity to negative evaluation, that leads to avoidance of social situations.

3. **Borderline Personality Disorder:** Emotional instability, unstable interpersonal relationships, rapid and intense mood swings; Instability with self-image, and relationships with a tendency towards impulsivity and fear of abandonment.

4. **Dependent Personality Disorder:** Excessive need to be taken care of leading to submissiveness, clinging behaviors, fear of abandonment, struggle with independence, self-reliance, and have difficulty with making decisions independently.

5. **Histrionic Personality Disorder:** Rapid shifts in emotions, unpredictable, shallow expression of feelings, excessively seeks attention, thinks relationships are closer than they really are, superficial lacking genuine connection, dramatic speech with strong opinions, overly dramatic or theatrical, exaggerated behavior, may have inappropriate sexual or provocative behaviors.

6. **Narcissistic Personality Disorder:** Excessive need for admiration, a sense of self-importance, disregard for

others, lack of empathy, inability to handle criticism, sense of entitlement, grandiosity, callous, unemotional traits, disregard for others' feelings.

7. Obsessive-Compulsive Personality Disorder: Pattern of perfectionism, orderliness, and control. Preoccupied with order, fixated on rules, schedules, lists, and organization. Excessive devotion to work and have productivity often neglecting personal needs and social interactions. Inflexible, rigid, stubborn, struggle with compromise or accept alternative approaches. Struggle with trusting others and delegating tasks.

8. Paranoid Personality Disorder: Pervasive distrust and suspicion of others. Doubt loyalty, fearing exploit-tation, misinterpretation of situations, and tend to hold grudges.

9. Schizoid Personality Disorder: lack of interest in social relationships and prefer solitary activities with limited range of emotional expression.

10. Schizotypal Personality Disorder: Involves eccentric or odd behaviors and thoughts, unusual beliefs and have difficulty with socially interacting with others.

Personality disorders require a medical diagnosis and is treated with psychotherapy, also known as talk-therapy. A Christ-Centered and Biblical Psychotherapist can help individuals gain understanding and manage symptoms by giving foundational cognitive coping mechanisms that have a spiritual dimension nurturing the spirit of man or woman first to enlighten in truth, give hope, validate, comfort, and see things from a positive perspective. God's love is demonstrated to the person as the psychotherapist functions in gentleness, kindness, patience, self-control, mercy, grace, and with the *Spirit of Understanding*. The psychotherapist is driven with compassion, truth, boldness, assertiveness, and gentle care as the layers of developmental trauma is unraveled. As the Holy Spirit leads, the psychotherapist gives understanding as to how the client got to the state that they're in and helps the client understand their symptoms. Also, the psychotherapist helps the client understand how their behaviors affects others, reducing problematic behaviors. Usually, the gift of *word of wisdom* and *word of knowledge* is given by the Holy Spirit to the psychotherapist to deliver a definitive message from God in light of what the person is experiencing, thinking, or feeling.

God is made known to the client as the psychotherapist operates in these gifts. Oftentimes, the psychotherapist is given this revelatory insight that only God knew about that person who is being treated causing the client to experience the tangible power of God in His awesomeness! God's power is demonstrated to the client and the client identifies that God is indeed real and knows all things! Christ-Centered, Biblical, and Spiritual Psychotherapy helps introduce a new set of visual lenses to see things through the eyes of God versus themselves. People will no longer be driven by their emotional and psychological pain. Instead, they are conforming to truth and truth is what removes the distorted lens to see situations clearly. As I indicated earlier in this book, God is a *Spirit of Truth.* Therefore, when serving as *His Counselor,* and as a *Prophetic Counselor* guided by the *Spirit of Counsel* my job is to execute truth, love, hope, peace, clarity, understanding, validation, and healing.

Invalidation is one of the primary underlying root causes of unhealthy thought and behavioral patterns associated with past traumas and prolonged childhood trauma. These patterns can progress and develop into *personality disorders.* A survivor of abuse trauma often experiences the act of someone dismissing, rejecting, or denying their feelings, thoughts, and behavior. Invalidation makes an abuse trauma survivor feel unimportant, and devalued, or make it seem as if their feelings are wrong. Invalidation can be intentional or unintentional that is inflicted onto a person by another person which is a form of emotional abuse. Anger, shame, guilt, and worthlessness are some of the repressed feelings associated with the root system of invalidation. Mental illnesses and disorders are often traced back to underlying root systems of trauma that have never been processed or understood by the victim.

Trauma is like a tree with a root system. In the root system of the tree, you will see as I mentioned previously in this book thus far, various traumas. Some of these trauma's as mentioned before includes, sexual assault and rape, childhood sexual abuse, domestic violence, death, loss, natural disasters, war, fires, terrorism, violence, racial injustices, abuse: emotional, verbal, mental, spiritual, physical, sexual, etc. If trauma is left unresolved or unprocessed the tree will grow up sick with branches that represent various symptoms of mental illnesses that if not detected by a skilled Psychotherapist can be clinically misdiagnosed or labeled wrong as a Mental Illness that is not conducive to what they are truly experiencing. Some of these mental health related issues; symptoms and disorders include:

- Depression
- Panic Attacks
- Anxiety
- Detachment
- Dissociation
- Poor Concentration; ADHD
- Hypersensitivity
- Hypervigilance
- Promiscuity
- Body Image issues
- Insomnia
- PTSD
- PTSD Amnesia
- Flashbacks
- Depersonalization: Persistent feeling from outside one's body or having a sense that one's

surrounding isn't real.

- Delusions

Some of these mental health related issues are driven by fear. God's word tells us that, ***"For God has not given us a spirit of fear; but of power, and of love, and of a sound mind." – 2 Timothy 1:7, NKJV.***

A traumatic event, a crisis, and other difficult life situations causes fear as a normal response to a life-threatening situation, danger, and uncertainty associated with the traumatic event experienced. Although, fear is a normal human emotion and human response it does not have dominance over God's power! God's power is greater than fear! God's love overrides fear! ***"There is no fear in love, but perfect love casts out fear…" – 1 John 4:18, NKJV.*** Love is what makes a human being feel safe and secure. The human brain is wired for security and safety. Love is the healing virtue and power that enhances security and a sound mind. God is love (1 John 4:8). Anyone that is in God and God is in them also walks in love. A *Prophetic Counselor* or *Christ-Centered Psychotherapist* is driven by love to bring hope and healing to the lives that have been appointed to them to help.

To have good mental health is to have soundness of the mind. A sound mind is what God gives us. Soundness of the mind is to think clearly, rationally, have under-standing, and to make healthy decisions. Mental clarity is what God provides when you are willing to receive His counsel. God's counsel helps you to understand situations and information clearly without confusion or delusion. The Holy Bible declares, *God is not the author of confusion.*

"For God is not the author of confusion, but of peace, as in all churches of the saints." – 1 Corinthians 14:33, NKJV. Jesus helps you to reason contributing to rational thinking to make logical decisions not based on emotions. God increases our mental capacity and enhances our cognitive function. ***"Blessed be to the Lord, who daily loads us with benefits, even the God of our salvation. Selah." – Psalms 68:19, NKJV.***

When you face depression which involve symptoms such as: suffering from hopelessness, sleepless nights or excessive sleep, lack of energy-motivation to engage in activities, no interest in pleasure or activities, fatigue, restlessness, apathy, lack of appetite, weight loss, increase of appetite, weight gain, repetitive thoughts, mood swings, sadness, poor concentration, agitation, irritability, and suicidal ideations, rest assure that *God is the lifter of your head,* (Psalms 3:3). When you are suffering from anxiety, which is a natural human response to internal stressors or a trauma response to unprocessed trauma, God gently reminds us that we don't have to be anxious. Instead, we can *look to the hills which comes our help, our help comes from the Lord* (Psalms 121:1). Therefore, you shift your mind from anxiety; excessive worry, and you go to God in prayer, petitioning God what you need by presenting your requests to God, thanking Him in faith, believing that He is going to answer you in His timing and respond His way. ***"Be anxious for nothing, but in everything by prayer and supplication, with thanksgiving, let your requests be made known to God." – Philippians 4:6, NKJV.*** One of the ways He responds to you is making Himself available through the *Spirit of Counsel*. Seeking Godly counsel is certainly His Will! Again, as mentioned before, there is protection in counseling (Proverbs 11:14), and when you do not seek counseling, your mind will cease to function appropriately.

You have to lay aside any unrealistic expectations and yield to Gods ways not what you want, or think is best for you. This is allowing Jesus to be Lord over your mental health and your overall health. True healing comes when you submit to His authority and yield to His ways. In His authority and sovereignty, God, the Father gives the *Doctor's Orders* and makes decisions that are in alignment with His plan and purpose for your life. God always knows what's best for you and your life because He created you and He knows the plans and purposes that He has for you and your life.

Jesus, *Yeshua* is the *Peace Giver* because He is the *Prince of Peace* (Isaiah 9:6). God is *"Jehovah Shalom, The Lord is our Peace."* Jesus brings harmony to our life. He gives us peace which is the state of tranquility and freedom from disturbances and conflict within ourselves and in life. Peace is the calm that silences the racing, intrusive-repetitive thoughts, uncertainties, confusion, and lack of understanding in the human mind. Jesus is our Healer, and He uses strategy to heal. Jesus takes action that is designed to achieve the overall aim to heal.

As you seen throughout this chapter, and thus far reading this book, God is a dimensional and multifaceted God. He is limitless! God is marvelous in everything He does, and He is perfect in all His ways!

God just doesn't heal in one fashion or way. He brings about healing in so many multifaceted ways. Healing comes in the form of supernatural power. Healing also comes by His spoken word declared. Yet, healing still comes in other forms that remains just as miraculous through the utilization of His people in their creative innovation, professional expertise, gifts, wisdom and knowledge, skills, talents that ALL come from God alone. Healing also comes by utilizing God's creative natural elements found on the earth, whether it is medication, the practice of medicine, or holistic medicines such as organic superfoods dietary supplements, relaxation and mindfulness, chiropractic, massage therapy, nutrition and wholefoods, herbal medicines, exercise and stretching healing body movements, mind and body interventions, meditation, etc. God created it ALL!

God also gives the ultimate healing which is eternal healing that comes when our spirit departs from the physical body. The ultimate healing comes when we enter Heaven following the death of the physical body on earth and being resurrected to a new life in eternity. Let's not limit God but embrace this truth! Jesus heals as He sees fit in every unique situation and with each individual because He is the *Great Physician*!

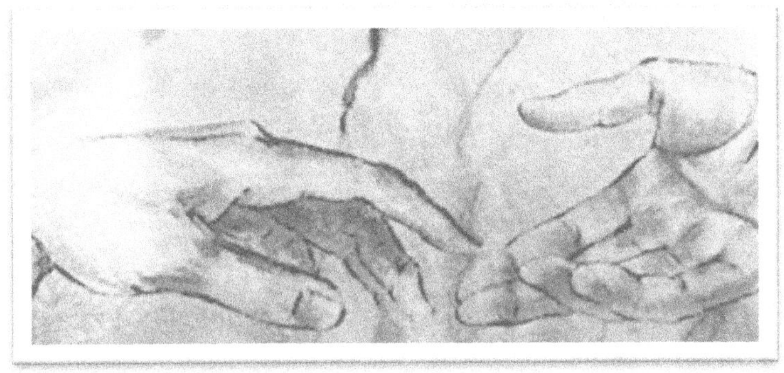

Chapter 5: The Prince of Peace

You were created to experience true peace in this life that only comes from God, who is *Jehovah Shalom* meaning, *The Lord is Peace*, and Yeshua, Jesus, *The Prince of Peace.*

Jesus speaks to us in scripture, ***"Peace I leave with you, My peace I give unto you: not as the world gives do I give to you. Let not your heart be troubled, neither let it be afraid." – John 14:27, NKJV.*** The meaning of the Hebrew word, *Shalom,* means to be safe, sound, healthy, and unscathed. Also, *Shalom* means to be at peace, to be finished or completed, uninjured in mind and body. To experience *Jehovah Shalom*, is to have a sense of well-being and harmony, to be in good health, wholeness, acquire happiness, quietness of the soul, preservation, prosperity, contentment, tranquility, security, and safety.

I want to take a moment and pray for you:

Father, I pray now in the name of Jesus for the person reading this book. I decree now that the peace of God rules your heart. I speak Shalom *over you. Father, give them peace that surpasses all understanding. Father, shower Your peace that cancels out fear, worry, defeat, and hopelessness. I declare that the* Prince of Peace *come to you now and give you rest. I decree that you will no longer be weary. I declare that you will rise up in a new strength, in Jesus' name!*

Father, embrace your son or daughter with your peace, comfort, and love. I declare soundness and clarity over your mind. Lord, help them to trust you with all their heart, and lean not to their own understanding as Your Word says in Proverbs 3:5. I declare that you will acknowledge God in all your ways and as you do this the Lord will direct your path according to Proverbs 3:6.

I declare that you are strong in the Lord and have the mind of Christ according to 1 Corinthians 2:16. I pray now that the peace of God overshadows you, cover you at all times, and guard you. I cancel out anxiety, depression, and heaviness right now, in Jesus Name! I declare that you are more than a conqueror in Christ Jesus! I bind condemnation, and loose truth and hope over your mind. I declare over you, "Therefore, there is no condemnation to those who are in Christ Jesus," according to Romans 8:1. I bind shame and guilt and loose forgiveness, mercy, and grace over you. I declare that you will walk in freedom to be all that God created you to be, in Jesus Name! I decree that the Lord will make His face shine upon you and give you joy unspeakable.

Father, by Your anointing, I break every stronghold and destroy every yoke in the life of the person reading this book right now, in Jesus Name! Every mental stronghold, soul tie, generational curse, and lie be broken now, chains of bondage be broken now, by the power and anointing of Jesus Christ! Lord, expel darkness out of their life, close doors that have disrupted peace and every principality, and spirit of wickedness be gone now in Jesus Name! Father, let the light of your Glory penetrate their heart, mind, soul, and spirit right now, in Jesus Name! Amen.

Now, you may be or have been experiencing some difficult circumstances. Perhaps, you have experienced troubling experiences in the past that has impacted you in a negative way. However, I am here to tell you that this is your time to heal and reclaim your identity and life! To reclaim your life is to focus on self-reflection, explore what's valuable to you, your interests, set boundaries, embrace new experiences, seek counsel, support, and cultivate self-care. God would have not led me to pray over you just a moment ago. You are on the Father's mind! That's why you are holding and reading this book right now. God speaks *Shalom* over you right now. You were never meant to live in despair and defeat. God is telling you to *look up,* because your help comes from Him. When you look up, posturing your spirit to lean into God who is your strength and joy in the midst of chaos, you will receive hope and reassurance. When you spiritually position yourself in pursuit of God you will receive a peace that is too good to articulate with words. It's a peace that sustains you, holds you together, comforts you, encourages you, and gives you a will to keep persevering in the face of life difficulties.

I am a living testament of this peace that I am talking about. I was once hopeless, felt defeated, and didn't have the strength to carry on. Yet, I encountered the *Peace Giver* and the *Peacekeeper*. Jesus met me in every trial throughout my life in every season. Jesus carried me, took me by the hand, and led me through every valley that I was destined to walk through. You were never meant to do life alone. Although, you may have felt all alone in life. You were never alone. God tells us in His word, that *He will never leave us nor forsake us, and He goes with us* (Deuteronomy 31:6). Have you ever just thought about all that you have encountered in your life that was downright hard. Think about all that has happened to you and how you are still living, breathing, and moving. That my friend is the miracle that we often underestimate or don't perceive as a miracle. It is God's grace that is upholding you and preserving you.

As you trust in the Lord, hope will arise, and peace that settles all doubts, fears, and uncertainties, will come. ***"May the God of hope fill you with all joy and peace as you trust Him." – Romans 15:13, NKJV.*** To encounter the peace of God we must learn to *be still* and know that God is who He says He is (Psalm 46:10). You may ask, what does it mean to *be still*? This is a spiritual posture when you are cognizant in choosing to fix your mind on God being all supreme power over every situation you face in life. To trust God is to believe in God's reliability, and love. To trust God is simply placing your life and every aspect of your life in His hands. To trust God entails having faith in His Word and promises which are concrete, and absolute. The promises of God are *yes and amen,* meaning that they will be so according to what He has proclaimed in His written and spoken word, the Holy Bible. Trusting God is to put total confidence in Him even when your feelings or circumstances might lead you to believe otherwise.

Psalm 34:15 (NKJV) states, ***"…Seek peace and pursue it."*** Jesus is our *Peace Giver* and *Peacekeeper*. Yet, we must do our part and that is to seek peace out. Jesus is a gentleman. He will not force or give you something that you don't want, or not ready for. Therefore, you have to do your part in seeking God in an unrelenting pursuit. As you do this you will find the peace that you have always yearned for that you most certainly cannot obtain from anything in this world. You personally have to pursue the God of Peace. To pursue Jesus, you have to make Him first and desire to follow Him in order to receive the benefit of peace that He freely gives us when we seek after Him with our whole heart and mind. The Word of God says, ***"…seek ye first the Kingdom of God and His righteousness and all these things shall be added unto you." – Matthew 6:33, KJV***.

Everything that we have need of and sometimes

worry about in our human nature will be given to us if we seek God first. It is a spiritual principle and discipline to make God your number one priority, first love, and have an undeniable pursuit for Jesus, *His righteousness.* Seeking God and His righteousness is a command not an optional thing. Obedience is what it will take to follow His commands and you will reap peace as you walk in faith and in obedience to His precepts. Jesus tells us that, *if you love Me, you will obey My commands* (John 14:15).

Next, we have to let go of worry in order to obtain the peace of God. Now, worry is a valid emotion, and it is very real in our human nature. However, you must choose to walk in the Spirit and not in your human flesh or nature. You are allowed to express this feeling and acknowledge this feeling in your humanity, but do not let it lead you or control you. Instead, take your worry to God in prayer and petition to God to take it away in exchange for peace as you release worry to God. He then gives you peace in exchange to rule out worry and ease the anxiety that comes with worry. ***"Therefore, do not worry about tomorrow, for tomorrow will worry about its own things. Sufficient for the day is its own trouble." – Matthew 6:34, NKJV.***

Mindfulness is a therapeutic strategy to assist clients with practicing grounding techniques that ground you emotionally, psychologically, and even spiritually. This practice helps with managing anxiety, excessive worry, hypervigilance, and hypersensitivity which are symptoms of post-traumatic stress. Mindfulness engages clients to learn how to engage their five senses; sight, smell, hearing, tasting, and touching to ground oneself in the here and now. The goal is to ground yourself in the present moment shifting your focus from stressors, pain, triggers, anxiety, worry, depression, and post-traumatic stress that often disrupt ability to function. Rather, you are learning to focus on what is good, peaceful, tranquil, and what's happening in the present moment and embracing the moment. There is a blessing in the moment, and it is important that we learn to embrace every moment that is allotted to us. I often say, *time is of the essence and time is one thing that you cannot get back, so it is vital that you don't miss the blessing in the now.* Peace comes when you choose not to dwell or ponder on the past and what you cannot change. Also, peace comes when you choose to not worry about the future that produces fear. Instead, focus on the blessing in the now.

I am going to take a moment and talk about a *peacemaker* and how the role of a *peacemaker* as a Christ-Centered Counselor or Psychotherapist can have a huge impact on a person's life when providing counseling and psychotherapy. Jesus states in the Holy Bible, ***"Blessed are the peacemakers, for they will be called sons of God." – Matthew 5:9, NKJV.***

Proverbs 16:7 (NKJV) states, "When a man's ways please the Lord, He makes even his enemies to be at peace with him." As a son or daughter of God, who carries the *Prince of Peace* inside of them, they are a *peacemaker* who sows in peace and reaps a harvest. The *peacemaker* has been given favor with not only God but with man. Therefore, when I am providing Christ-centered, Biblical counseling, and psychotherapy I am sowing words of peace that bring calmness, clarity, and a gift from God that surpasses human understanding. I am giving Godly understanding under the influence and inspiration of the Holy Spirit causing the person to see things that once was in the dark to now seeing in a new light. This allows for the Holy Spirit to be *The Great Comforter* to alleviate and even totally eliminate the distress of the person who is receiving counseling or psychotherapy.

As a Counselor of light who carries the Glory of the Lord imparts peace into the lives of those who seek God in counseling. I truly believe that as God's Counselor I am a carrier of hope, glory, and light. That in itself is an awesome privilege and responsibility that I must steward well to continue to be an effective conduit for God's Spirit and Glory to flow through. I believe that as God's Counselor I am a channel of God's healing power. God causes His people to lie down and sleep in His peace and live in safety (Psalms 4:8).

Insomnia is a common mental health issue and symptom of various mental disorders. Sleep deprivation is a serious problem that leads to so many other medical related issues and spiritually it is a tactic of the enemy of your soul to rob you of sleep. Sleep is what repairs cells and regenerates new cells in your body. Sleep also regenerates new brain cells. Sleep helps new neurons to grow in the brain that help enhance cognition and the executive region of the brain to think sharper, faster, and reason effectively. Sleep regenerates cells in the brain and throughout the entire body supporting every system in the body promoting good overall health. I am here to tell you now, that God will grant you sleep. It is one of His promises in the Word of God, "***When you lie down, you will not be afraid; Yes, you will lie down and your sleep will be sweet." – Proverbs 3:24, NKJV.***

Jesus is "The Lily of the Valleys" (Song of Solomon 2:1). Spiritually speaking, valleys are not always a desirable place to be because it is a low place in life when you are facing great difficulties. However, naturally speaking, in the valley there is usually a river or stream flowing through the valley that nourishes, gives life to flowers that grow, and blossom in the valley. The beauty, vibrancy, color, fragrance often give a sweet aroma that instantly brings happiness, joy, and a sense of tranquility. This is what the holy scripture is referencing to Jesus being the *The Lily of the Valleys.* Notice, the scripture says, "Valleys," which is indicative that you will face not only one valley in your life but many valleys. Jesus is *The Living Water* that flows in the valley and brings peace in the valley causing you to grow and blossom in your valley season. Moreover, when you put your trust and hope in the God of Peace you will be kept in peace. It is in His peace that cradles us, covers us, and sustains us in every valley season. "***You will keep him in perfect peace, Whose mind is stayed on You, Because he trusts in You. Trust in the Lord forever, For YAH, the Lord is everlasting strength." – Isaiah 26:3-4, NKJV***.

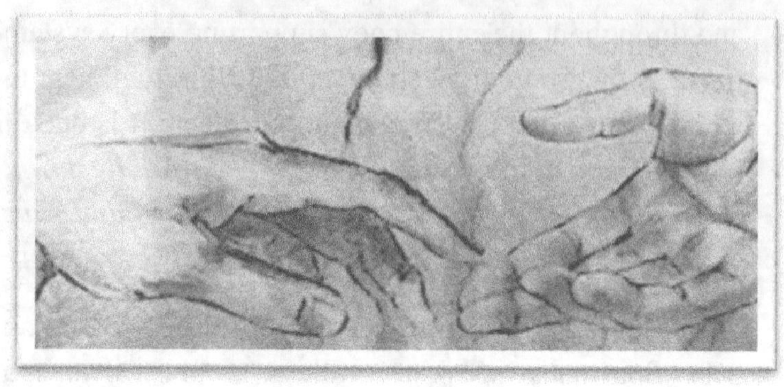

Chapter 6: A Sound Mind

"***Let this mind be in you, which was also in Christ Jesus." – Philippians 2:5, NKJV.***

God wants our minds healed! God not only wants us to heal spiritually. Moreover, God wants our minds healed! When our minds are healed our body can be healed and restored. As I indicated previously, the mind and body are interconnected. Counseling with Jesus involves a Counselor who not only has an academic background, clinical training, and skills, but who also has been anointed by God to activate the specific parts of the brain. A Counselor and Psychotherapist is an essential tool of God Almighty. A Counselor and Psychotherapist is clinically trained to bring stored information in the hippocampus of the brain to the pre-frontal lobe cortex which is the front executive system region of the brain responsible for: reasoning, judgement, organization, planning, impulse control, behavior, regulate emotions, empathy, attention, focus, learning from past mistakes, and problem-solving. A Counselor is able to help exercise the brain and the mind to rewire and change the course of how the brain has been conditioned to malfunction.

Oftentimes, the hippocampus, part of the limbic system, is left to fend for itself or left in an overload state that plays a key role in depression and could potentially cause shrinkage of the hippocampus that primarily leads to cognitive impairments such as: memory loss, problems with forming new memories, spatial navigation difficulties; cognitive processing, coordinating behavior, language, attention, memory, perceiving environment, and overall cognitive decline often associated with Alzheimer's disease and depression. The shrinking of the hippocampus can affect your ability to learn and recall information effectively. The hippocampus is the region in the back of the brain in the temporal lobe responsible for consolidating short-term memories into long-term memories, learning, and forming memory. The hippocampus is also responsible for forming mental maps of our environment and navigate spaces effectively.

There are a number of factors that cause shrinkage of the hippocampus. Aging as we all know is a common factor. However, I want to focus more on key factors of stress hormones, biological and neurobiological issues, lifestyle habits, and mental health related issues such as depression, and post-traumatic stress that are not so much understood as key factors to decline function of the hippocampus. Hippocampal shrinkage leads to cognitive deficits such as memory, change in cognitive function and increased risk of cognitive decline. Cognitive deficits are a malfunction of the mind. Poor lifestyle habits such as poor diet, alcohol consumption that is mood altering, lack of fitness levels in exercise, obesity, hypertension, etc. can all contribute to hippocampal atrophy, as well as depression and prolonged post-traumatic stress. Physical activity is key in promoting brain health and increasing hippocampal volume. Depression can cause changes in the hippocampus's plasticity. Antidepressants can stimulate neurogenesis and reverses the inhibitory effects of stress on the hippocampus as little as 3-4 weeks.

Let's take a moment and talk more about one of the leading mental illnesses in the world today which is depression. Over 280-million people are living with depression, including 23-million children and adolescents (World Health Organization, www.who.int). Now, as humans we all experience sadness, sorrow, despair, emotional, and psychological suffering. However, what happens when these feelings are persistent and remain for a prolonged period? Stress is a major risk factor for depression that can cause the brain to be exposed to corticosteroids which can downregulate hippocampal neurogenesis which is the process of new neurons that are formed in the brain to enhance human function, and directly influence neuronal activity. Growing up in a dysfunctional family system or experiencing childhood maltreatment is prevalent in people with depression.

For example, a person who grew up in a home with an authoritarian parent who was controlling, rigid, insensitive, non-empathetic, and ruled with an iron fist to enforce obedience is more susceptible to developing depression. Perhaps, the authoritarian parent was spiritually abusive, emotionally negligent, emotionally, and verbally abusive. A person who grew up in this type of authoritarian parental family system may experience the need for perfectionism or struggle with perfectionism always living under a built in self-induced internal measuring scale. The person may never feel good enough, competent, or adequate. Low self-worth can stem from an authoritarian parenting style family system that contributes to the development of depression over time.

Depression is characterized by persistent depressed mood or loss of interest in activities causing impairment in daily living. *Adverse Childhood Experiences* are key contributing factors to the development of depression as well as a series of complex traumatic events throughout the human life span. Often, a psychotherapist or counselor that specializes in mental health or trauma-focused counseling and therapy utilizes the *Adverse Childhood Experiences* (ACES, 1998 & 2004. *See Appendix B in the back of book per source citation*) assessment tool to help identify the underlying root causes of depression or stress-related disorders. Current unhealthy behaviors and psychological issues usually stem from adverse experiences that has happened to a person at some point in the person's life that was too difficult for them to cope with.

The Psychotherapist/Counselor engages client in processing contributing factors to depression through cognitive processing therapy, trauma-focused therapies that involve prolonged exposure therapy, inner child work, conducting a trauma timeline review, trauma-focused cognitive behavioral therapy; trauma narrative, trauma reprocessing, cognitive coping, psychoeducation, desensitization, and so forth. These are some of the various psychological therapies that I practice as a Qualified Mental Health Professional (QMHP). However, there are other therapies that are effective in treating depression. Psychodynamic psychotherapy is another effective therapy that I often practice where I encourage the client to say whatever is going through their mind and look at how childhood experiences affect the person's thinking, feelings, and behaviors. The goal is to create a safe and supportive environment where people can explore their traumatic memories, internal stressors, develop healthy coping skills, and work toward a successful recovery. There are many other forms of psychotherapies that are effective. However, these are some of the therapies that are very effective in the treatment for depression, post-traumatic stress, and other mental disorders.

God knew from the beginning that in this life people

would suffer emotionally, mentally, physically, and even spiritually. However, with God being who He is and always was the GREAT I AM, had a master plan. This master plan consists of restoration, divine healing, reconciliation, grace, and hope! I love what the Word of God says in 1 Peter 5:10 (NASB), ***"And after you have suffered a little while, the God of all grace, who called you to eternal glory in Christ, will Himself perfect, confirm, strengthen, and establish you."*** This scripture verse is a reminder that God is going to do something with the tragedy, trauma, loss, and crisis situation that you may be currently facing or have faced in your life.

I am a firm believer that nothing we experience in this life on earth is in vain nor is anything wasted. God uses all of the pain, misfortune, failures, shortcomings, and trials that you encountered along the journey of life for your good. Everything that we experience in life whether good or bad there is a lesson to be learned. There is an opportunity for growth and change in all the life experiences we encounter. We can choose to grow bitter or better. I personally, chose to grow better on many occasions where life dealt me a bad hand or life curves throughout my life journey. I look back and reflect on the past 48 years of my life here on earth, and I can honestly say that I could have easily given up on life many times due to the various traumas, trials, and tribulations. However, something inside of me wouldn't let me. *That something is God,* my Sustainer whose strength was made perfect when I was weak and when I didn't have the strength to carry on. God is certainly the *Author and the Finisher of my Faith* (Hebrews 12:2) just as the Holy Bible declares.

As I sit here and think, writing this book, allowing myself to be totally transparent and vulnerable, I can see that God from the beginning, always had a master plan for my life. Who would have thought that once upon a time a little multiracial girl with an African American, German, and Native American racial ethnicity who grow up in a broken family system of divorced parents living in poverty in a single parent home with a single mother who did the best she could raising 3 children on her own would one day prosper? Who would have imagined that this broken girl who had unknown resiliency would one day become an Entrepreneur, a Founder and Counseling Business Owner, Pastor, Speaker, Counselor and Psychotherapist, Book Writer, Author, and Publisher? How could this broken girl who once had insecurities associated with so much experienced complex traumas, adverse childhood experiences, loss, hurt, mental and emotional distress throughout her childhood and lifetime could persevere through it all and come out victoriously? God had it thought out way before the foundations of this world! God knew from the beginning what His plan was for my life. Jeremiah 29:11 (NKJV) says it best, ***"For I know the thoughts that I think toward you, says the Lord, thoughts of peace and not of evil, to give you a future and a hope."***

I share this with you as the reader to let you know that God is able, and He most certainly will restore your mental health, emotional health, physical health, and spiritual health if you come to Him and allow Him to do His healing work in your life. I recall when I returned to the Lord at the age of 23 after running astray from the Lord for quite some time. I had initially given my heart to Jesus as a little girl and was baptized at the age of 15. However, at 23 years old I had gotten to a rock-bottom place of despair. At that time, I was in a deep state of depression, married for 3 years, had 3 children all under the age of 5, a college student, working part-time, and had so much unprocessed childhood trauma that was crippling me emotionally and psychologically. However, at the time I didn't realize what it was, nor did I understand trauma. Although, I was going to college and majoring in Social Work, then later earning a Master of Arts Degree in Trauma Counseling, little did I know what I was learning in college was what I was going to have to walk through. I had to apply what I was learning to unpack my personal childhood trauma and heal.

I will never forget that early Sunday morning when I rededicated my life to Jesus. I was visiting my mother and I had spent the night. At the break of dawn, I heard an audible voice calling my name several times, *"Tina, Tina, Tina."* Finally, knowing immediately that this was God's voice, I responded. I was instructed by God to get up, get dressed, and go to the church that I had never been to, nor did I know where the church was. I was then instructed to call my paternal grandmother, who was a Pastor at the time who lived not too far from my mother's home, to inquire about this church. God instructed me to obtain the directions to the church from my grandmother in which He was telling me to go to. I knew without a doubt that this was most certainly God's voice! I could feel the tangible presence of God and I just had an absolute knowing in my spirit. As I got dressed, I decided to go to my grandmother's house that Sunday morning rather than call her to get the directions to this church where I was instructed to go. I remember the smile my grandmother had on her face. It was as if she knew exactly what God was doing and that He was at work in my life. As I gave her the name of the church, she knew precisely where it was and gave me directions to get there, which was 45 minutes away. In fact, my grandmother personally knew the Pastor of the church whom she was also friends with.

I left her home en route to the church. As I arrived at the church, I felt a warm and loving presence in the parking lot. I instantly felt peace. I began to cry. When I approached the church and entered, I was greeted with such love by the people at the church. I sat in the back of the church. The church was rather large. I began to observe and listened attentively to the worship and preaching. Suddenly, it was as if God Himself was speaking directly to me through the Pastor whom I had never met. The Pastor had no idea who I was and what I was going through. However, he was reading my mail and knew exactly everything about me and what I was currently going through. So much so that he began to operate in the gift of *Word of Wisdom*, *Word of Knowledge*, and *Prophecy*.

Toward the end of his message, the Pastor

proceeded to say these words, "There is a young woman in here today and you came for the first time, you've been very depressed, and God Himself has called you today and ordained for you to be here in this church right now, today."

The Pastor then said (and I am paraphrasing simply because this was nearly 25 years ago), "Woman, today is your day, God is going to heal you and put you on a path that He has chosen for you, and you will never be the same from this day forth."

The next thing I know, I am at the altar wailing out loud in tears from the pit of my soul and the Pastor laid his hands on my head and prayed over me. I then began praying in an unknown, heavenly language, as I was being baptized in the Holy Spirit. My spirit was conversing with God. Although, I had experienced the power of the Holy Spirit when I initially gave my life to Jesus as a child, this encounter was much deeper than I have ever experienced. I can see it very clearly right now as if it was yesterday. In fact, I remember what I had on that day, a black summer dress with a white flower print.

This moment is etched in my mind forever. This was the day, in the year 2000, that God personally called me forth out of my pit of despair and began His work in me to transform my mind. He led me into a slow gradual process of obtaining a *sound mind.* Now, when I say a "slow gradual process," I mean it took years in the process of me doing much trauma work and developing my relationship with God to get to where I am today at the age of 48 years old. This church God led me to at the time would be the place where God began His sanctification process. This was the process of change as I was laying down my life to pick up my cross to follow after Jesus. God began to show me who I was in the Kingdom of God, at this church where my husband and I attended for seven years. God showed me that I was called to the ministry. He was establishing me after the years that I had suffered as a child and adolescent until my young adult years. The God of grace called me to His eternal glory in Christ, *perfected, confirmed, strengthened, and established* me just as what I previously mentioned as 1 Peter 5:10 proclaims. I remember from that day forward when I returned to Jesus, I was so full of joy, strength, and faith. I literally felt the heavy weight of despair, depression, shame, low self-worth, and hopelessness lift off of me. I was on an uphill climb! My husband and I later became Licensed Ministers/Pastors in this particular church organization.

Although, I arrived at a place of hope, spiritual growth, and healing, God was yet equipping me for so much more that was yet to come in my life. God knew the path that I was on was going to have many more valleys to endure in the future. Indeed, did I experience many more great valleys of pain and suffering. Especially, the worst traumatic event and tragedy that I never imagined that I would face at the age of 41 years old, in 2018, when I tragically lost my only son in a car accident. I never got the chance to say goodbye to him. One minute my beloved son was here and the next he was gone, just like that. Again, I would face hopelessness, despair, depression, unbearable emotional, mental, spiritual, and even physical pain all associated with traumatic grief.

Matthew 5:34 (NIV) states, ***"Daughter, your faith has healed you. Go in peace and be freed from your suffering."*** I had to realize in my suffering of loss, tragedy, and traumatic grief that I had to reach for Jesus, lean into Him, take His hand as I have always done in every valley season experienced in my lifetime. I had to exercise my faith and believe with everything in me that God was going to bring me out just as He has from all the other afflictions in my life. "***Many are the afflictions of the righteous but God delivers him out of them all." – Psalm 34:19, NKJV.*** God doesn't just deliver you from one difficult situation, He delivers you out of them ALL! God delivered Jesus, who was righteous, from the many afflictions. Jesus, who walked this earth as God manifested in flesh, was delivered from afflictions. The afflictions Jesus endured were rejection, persecution, betrayal, false accusations, and ill-treatment. Jesus also experienced loss when Joseph, his earthly father, who raised Him, along with Mary, who conceived Jesus by the Holy Spirit. Jesus was afflicted with the mental distress of knowing that He would be killed in the crucifixion on the cross for the sins of the world for all mankind as His divine purpose that was assigned to Jesus by God, the Father. Jesus was afflicted with the deep anguish of feeling like God, the Father abandoned and forsaken Him on the cross of Calvary to the point where

He cried out to God, "Father why have you forsaken me!" (Matthew 27:46). God shared in our humanity by becoming flesh and walked among us through His only begotten Son, Jesus.

Therefore, God understands depression and He has a strategy to heal all those who have lost hope, and those who are currently experiencing or who have experienced deep anguish of the soul. Isaiah 53:4 (NASB) states, ***"However, it was our sicknesses that He Himself bore. And our pains that He carried: Yet we ourselves assumed that He had been afflicted, struck down by God, and humiliated."*** That strategy is empathy, validation, normalization of feelings and allowing expression of emotional reactions as it relates to real, human, painful life experiences. This strategy happens when a Counselor/Psychotherapist is relational with the client through talk-therapy in a healthy professional therapeutic relationship. God understands us in our humanity that we must have the freedom to express our emotions freely without any shame or guilt.

God wants us to be understood, valued, and respected. God empathizes with us. He feels what you feel and understands without any judgment what you are feeling. God extends mercy, grace, and love to us. I recall the horrific day when I lost my son, and I had a supernatural encounter with Jesus. Jesus came to me in an open vision, and He looked me in my eyes. What I remember the most when our eyes locked, was the gentle, warm, peaceful, loving, caring, empathetic, and yet very powerful looking eyes. Jesus looked at me with understanding and sadness. He was feeling my pain but, with reassurance. Jesus was letting me know that He knew exactly what I was feeling in my sorrow. He hated what I was feeling and experiencing. However, He was also letting me know that I was going to be okay and that my son was with him. In fact, as I have written in my book, *Pain to Purpose*, Porter, T. (2024), Jesus spoke these exact words to me, *"Your son has risen with Me."*

In counseling the Counselor and Psychotherapist ensures that the client is understood, valued, and respected through the process of facilitating open communication and expression of feelings. Emotions are meant to be regulated in a healthy way to identify and understand what you are feeling. When you choose to avoid, ignore what you are feeling, suppress or repress emotions which is unconsciously pushing down or ignoring feelings to avoid discomfort or emotional pain you experience emotional dysregulation that contributes to depression. When depressed, the amygdala neuron activity in the brain of encoding positive stimuli are less active and the neurons that encode negative stimuli are more active. Emotional dysregulation is when a person is unable to identify what they are feeling nor know how to express it or often display a flat emotional affect, unable to show any emotion.

Soundness of the mind comes when you choose to acknowledge that you are not okay, identify and openly express your feelings. A *sound mind* comes when you choose to activate your faith in something greater than yourself, your situation, and this life. That something greater is your Creator, your God and Father who takes away your heaviness and despair and gives you *beauty for ashes, joy for despair*, and wraps you up with the *garment of praise* for the *spirit of heaviness* (Isaiah 61:3). When you come to the Father in humility and faith, God gives you in exchange, a *Sound Mind*. To have a sound mind is to be free from mental illness, with the ability to adjust to daily life and feel comfortable with oneself and with others. God wants us to be sensible, well-balanced, sober with the ability to make good judgment and have wise discretion.

I want to take a moment and discuss the power of the mind and how an unhealthy mind can lead to bio-psycho-social issues such as psychosomatic disorder that I briefly mentioned previously in the book. Psycho-somatic is the connection between the mind and body. Often, mental health professionals refer to the bio-psycho-social model that suggest that biological, psychological, and social factors interact in complex ways to contribute to the development of illnesses or diseases as well as interfere with quality of life. Mental stress is a key factor in the idea that cause or worsen physical conditions. Psychosomatic disorders may cause psychosomatic syndromes associated with mental stress of pondered or repetitive thoughts and beliefs. Some of these psychosomatic syndromes include fibromyalgia, chronic fatigue, and irritable bowel syndrome. Treatments for psychosomatic disorders may include medication, psychotherapy, and stress relieving treatments.

Hypochondria is a serious mental disorder that develops progressively throughout time as a maladaptive behavior driven by fear and paranoia that could be brought on by having prolonged psychosomatic symptoms. Symptoms include long-term intense fear of having a serious condition and worry that minor symptoms indicate something serious. People who suffer in the mind to this magnitude are held captive to fear and paranoia. This fear and paranoia can be fueled by repeated thoughts and cause a person who is struggling with hypochondriac behaviors may visit doctors frequently or switch medical providers on a regular basis. The driving force of hypochondria is fear that leads to excessive worry and even panic attacks.

Compulsive behavior, dizziness or sensation of pin and needles in the body are common with hypochondria syndrome. As I mentioned earlier, *God has not given us a spirit of fear, but of power and of love and of a sound mind* (2 Timothy 1:7). God does not instill fear in us. Rather, He empowers and secures us with His love to have self-control instead. We are not to be ruled by fear. Rather, we are to rely on the strength and love God provides which leads to a *sound mind.*

Let's take a moment and look into other indicators of an unhealthy mind that are mental disorders. A psychosocial disorder is a mental illness that develops when a person's cognitive (mind) or behavioral processes are out of balance or due to difficult life experiences. Some examples of psychosocial disorders are *anxiety disorders such as panic attacks, obsessive compulsive disorder, post-traumatic stress disorder, agoraphobia; the fear of places and situations that cause panic, helplessness, or embarrassment, and social phobia.* Mood disorders such as, depression, bipolar, and dysthymic depression are other examples of psychosocial disorders. Other psychosocial disorders include, eating disorders such as anorexia and bulimia; psychotic disorders such as schizophrenia and schizo-affective disorder; addiction, and substance abuse such as alcoholism and drug addiction.

A person suffering from a psychosocial disorder is experiencing the functional impact and barriers similar to someone with a mental health related issue that is psychosocial. Psychosocial issues involve when a person is negatively impacted by the interactions with a social environment that is a barrier to their equality with others. Cognitive Behavioral Therapy is an effective counseling and therapy practice in treating psychosocial disorders to improve the patterns of thinking and alleviate the toxicity of negative thinking fueled by fear, paranoia, excessive worry, and anxiety. Interpersonal psychotherapy is also another effective therapy that I often use with a client who struggles with psychosocial disorders which helps the individual understand themselves and how they interact with others in their environment and improve relationships with others.

Throughout the years of my career in the helping profession, I have had the privilege to attain some of the most amazing clinical trainings from some of the best experts in the field of mental health, trauma, and clinical psychology around the world. Also, I can honestly say, where I obtained my Master of Art Degree specializing in Trauma and Crisis Response Counseling at Liberty University, I have partaken in great research studies about the many various aspects of neuroscience, trauma, psychology, and mental health. With that being said, Psychoanalysis is a method I have learned to apply when providing psychological therapy. Psychoanalysis is a practice method used by a psychotherapist to search through a person's subconscious memories to understand the source of their current difficulties, rather than focus on their conscious memories. The sub-conscious mind is not aware of the current thoughts, feelings, and behaviors associated with the past experiences that conditioned the mind to receive, process, interpret, and reason a certain way that may be misconstrued, inaccurate, or untrue. However, the perception is distorted subconsciously and often becomes the reality of that person. When providing this type of psychotherapy, I often meet with my clients who are receiving this type of therapy on a more frequent and consistent basis. The reason for more frequent counseling/therapy sessions is having the goal in mind to change the trajectory of the client's cognition to enhance healthier thought and behavioral patterns.

Using psychoanalytic techniques, the psycho-therapist will observe and analyze an individual's free associations, memories, and sometimes the person's dreams. Ideally, the psychotherapist will be non-judgmental. The goal of the psychotherapist is to help the person uncover their unconscious. The practice of psychoanalysis may interpret dreams to get insight into the workings of the person's unconscious mind. In the Bible, dream interpretation is essential. According to the Bible, interpretating dreams is often seen as a direct communication from God as it relates to significant events or future happening that is revealed through a person's dreams. Dreams are one way God speaks to us. In the Bible, God used Joseph to interpret Pharoah's dream to predict what is to come in the future. God was warning Pharoah and even sent His messenger to confirm what He was saying and what He would do to Egypt.

Likewise, when chosen, called, and anointed by God to be His messenger to give Counsel, direction, confirmation, and prophetic revelatory insight, "God's Counselor," or *Prophetic Counselor,* will do the same thing when providing counseling/psychotherapy under the *Spirit of Counsel.* In today's society, therapists generally view dreams as a reflection of an individual's subconscious mind, anxieties, desires, current emotional states, and unresolved, internal conflicts. Modern therapy focuses on the individual's personal experiences, and internal processes, to understand dream imagery. Dream analysis is a tool that today's therapist uses to explore deeper aspects of the psyche. Whereas, when operating under the *Spirit of Counsel*, God will enable the psychotherapist to interpret dreams to give prophetic meaning helping the person obtain hope and reassurance! Both Biblical and modern therapy interpretations focus on symbolism. However, the meaning behind the symbols may differ based on the person's cultural and religious background, with the Bible providing a framework for interpreting symbolism in dreams. Both types of dream interpretation purpose are to access and understand the deeper layers of the mind, whether it be through divine revelation or psychological exploration. All psychotherapists who use psychoanalysis therapy are cautious and always consider the client's perspective never imposing their own beliefs onto the client.

As a Christian Counselor/Psychotherapist having worked in the secular industry of mental health, I can definitively say that there is a huge difference and distinguished way of practicing in the field of counseling and psychotherapy. Both are equally important as they both serve as agents of helping people get better and heal. As I said before, I am a firm believer that *All Knowledge and Wisdom* comes from God! Therefore, in saying this, God can even operate through an academically, clinically, skilled, and trained Counselor and Therapist or mental health professional who is not a Christian and does not practice Christian Counseling and Therapy, just as He can through a Christian Counselor and Psychotherapist. God is all powerful! We cannot limit God. If God can speak through a donkey (Numbers 22:28) as demonstrated in the Holy Bible, then God can most certainly use a non-Christian Counselor, without them even knowing it, when He is trying to help individuals heal on the journey of life. God is not a respecter of persons. He will do whatever is necessary to reach and help people! Because God absolutely loves people! He loves His creation, and desires for all to know Him, and to have a relationship with Him.

The difference between the two practicing disciplines is that the Christian Counselor and Psychotherapist is operating under the influence of the *Spirit of Counsel*, which is God's Spirit, the Holy Spirit. The Christian Counselor and Psychotherapist is Christ-Centered, driven by the compassion of Jesus Christ, Holy Spirit led, and operating in the gifts of the Holy Spirit. The Christian Counselor and Psychotherapist has a genuine and intimate relationship with God the Father, Son (Jesus), and the Holy Spirit. For that reason, the Christian Counselor and Psychotherapist will give Godly counsel coinciding with God's Holy Word, the Bible. Therefore, a Christian Counselor and Psychotherapist will incorporate Biblical Counsel in conjunction with psychological therapy and integrated with the Christian spiritual dimension of hearing God and speaking for God when providing care for individuals who are seeking counsel.

Psychodynamic psychotherapy is also another therapy that a Psychotherapist can practice, which is almost interchangeable with psychoanalytic psychotherapy. However, psychodynamic psychotherapy uses shorter treatment periods and less frequency of sessions. Psychodynamic psychotherapy is very effective for people who are self-reflective and desire to gain insight into themselves and their behavior. Some of the psychodynamic therapy practice methods include, exploring childhood experiences, and focusing on unconscious thoughts and feelings. A psychotherapist who practices psychodynamic psychotherapy will focus on the client's free associations, do a dream analysis, and engage client in transference interpretation. A Mental Health Professional who practices psychodynamic psychotherapy helps individuals understand their unconscious thoughts, feelings, and past experiences to identify reoccurring themes and patterns in their lives. The goal of psychodynamic psychotherapy is to help clients develop psychological skills that can lead to making better choices and promote long-term well-being. Psychodynamic psychotherapy is effective in treating depression, anxiety, pain, and relationships just to name a few issues.

So, now that you have seen how God works in ensuring we obtain a *sound mind* so we can function effectively at optimal mental health, I encourage you to take the time to examine your mind, heart, and ways. ***"Let us examine our ways, and let us return to the Lord." – Lamentations 3:40, NIV.***

I strongly believe the reason for God impressing on my heart to write this book is to urge people around the globe to come to the Creator and seek Him while you have a chance. God desires for you to be whole, not just physically in your body, or not just spiritually, but in your mind! Psalms 139:23-24 (NIV), in the Holy Bible, states, ***"Search me, God, and know my heart; test me and know my anxious thoughts. See if there is any***

offensive way in me, and lead me in the way everlasting." God wants us to pay attention to ourselves. He tells us in Proverbs 4:23 (NCV), ***"Be careful what you think, because your thoughts run your life."***

God wants us to understand the seriousness of our existence here on earth. We weren't just created to exist for nothing living complacent in this life without purpose. I believe this is the leading mental health problem for many people around the world. People not understanding who they are, what their purpose is, and why they exist on this earth leads to a mental health crisis and mental health issues. I believe when a person doesn't understand how they are to function and does not refer to the owner's manual, which is God and His Holy Bible, that person experiences a sense of disarray. The Holy Bible was written by men, who were inspired by God, to write the accounts of God throughout the ancient Biblical times, so that we may know and understand the nature of our God, the Creator of heaven and earth, the universe, mankind, and all living creatures.

Think about it, when we purchase a new car and do not refer to the owner's manual, we may not know how to operate all the features on the car that may hinder us from reaching our destination. So it is with our minds. If we do not understand in which our mind was created to function, nor understand that we have the mind of our God, we must go to Him to get instructions on how to access the mind and learn how to function. God will then help us to navigate through this life for which we were created and purposed. In 2 Corinthians 13:5 (NIV), it states, ***"Examine yourselves to see whether you are in the faith; test yourselves. Do you not realize that Jesus Christ is in you? —unless of course, you fail."***

"I the LORD search the heart and examine the mind, to reward each person according to their conduct, according to what their deeds deserve." – Jeremiah 17:10, NIV. Self-examination is crucial. Self-examination is a principle that God instructs us to do, as you can see in the scripture passages I have shared above. God leads us to identify issues that are occurring in our mind when we lack soundness of the mind. When we take the time to do some self-examination, deep soul searching, keening into our thought processes, recurring themes, and behavioral patterns, God helps us discover where we need to heal. Then, God leads us on the journey of obtaining a *sound mind.* Taking the time to examine your life is very necessary and should be an ongoing priority. I encourage you to find a place where you can be alone and think, reflect, and perhaps journal what you discover. I challenge you to go a little further and deeper by asking the Holy Spirit to open your eyes to see what is going on in your life. Being ready to see what God shows you with an open mind, bring all the malfunction, distorted thinking, and maladaptive behaviors to God in confession. As you take the initiative to do this, I guarantee, you will be on the path of obtaining a *Sound Mind*. God says to you today, ***"And you will seek Me and find Me, when you search for Me with all your heart." – Jeremiah 29:13, NKJV.***

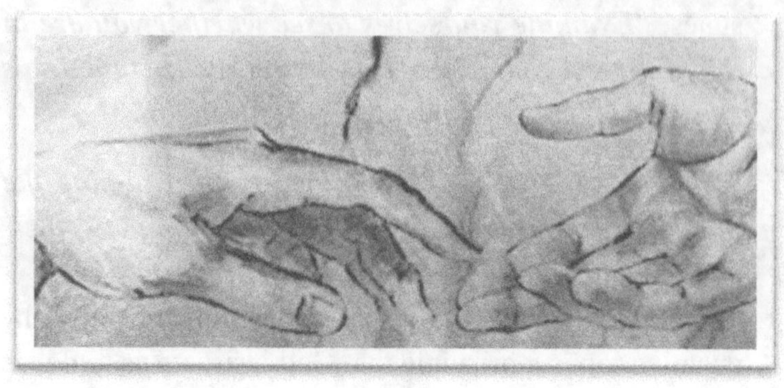

Chapter 7: God's Reboot of The Brain

The human brain is hardwired for God. ***"And from the throne proceeded lightnings, thunderings, and voices. Seven lamps of fire were burning before the throne, which are the sevenfold Spirit of God." – Revelation 4:5, NKJV.***

To understand God, His intricate, grandeur, and complex nature as well as His awesomeness, and extraordinary creative power we must understand things in the natural to understand God spiritually. After all, God is the creator of all things and *God is Spirit, and those who worship God must worship Him in spirit and in truth* (John 4:24). The Word of God proclaims that *Heaven is God's throne and earth is God's footstool* (Isaiah 66:1).

So, to lay the groundwork for this chapter let's

briefly delve into the principles of science. In the natural, according to NOAA, National Severe Storms Laboratory (.gov), lightning is a discharge of electricity that illuminates the sky. The National Weather Service (.gov) explains that lightning is made up of electrons that carry the electrical charge that produces the electrical event we see in the sky as a lightning bolt discharge that releases a substantial amount of energy. According to *Sharon's Weather Blog on www.kztv10.com—Why lightning is beneficial to plants*, Chief Meteorologist, Sharon Ray educates us on how the energy that comes from the lightning contributes to new plant growth due to the interaction with the atmospheric nitrogen and oxygen that forms nitrates which is a natural fertilizer booster that is provided to the soil carried by the rain. The lightning's energy can be calculated by measuring the length of a strike or it's voltage. However, Wikipedia, an online encyclopedia informs us that electrons have very small mass or matter that makes it a little more challenging to measure. Wikipedia indicates, matter is mass that can be weighed or measured by its volume, and it occupies space. However, electricity cannot be measured or weighed in the same way as matter (www.sciencefocus.com, Matthews, R. 2025).

Sounds a lot like God, doesn't it? God is the source of energy, life, and new growth! In God's infinite nature, He cannot be measured. In the same sense, just as lightning also ignites a shock wave that creates sound, which is what we hear after lightning strikes, creating a static charge, according to the National Weather Service

Government, that is the nature of things with God as well. Sound is produced by frequencies. The National Weather Service and National Oceanic and Atmospheric Administration provides us with education on how shock waves created by lightning expands explosively fast that turns into a sound of thunder that we hear in the sky. In the same way, so it is with God! God is all powerful and there is always a sound that proceeds from His throne that sends shock waves from Heaven's frequencies sending an electrical charge into the spiritual atmosphere on earth in which we inhabit as God's creation.

"For thus says the LORD Who created the heavens, Who is God, Who formed the earth and made it, Who has established it, Who did not create it in vain, Who formed it to be inhabited: I am the LORD, and there is no other." – Isaiah 45:18, NKJV.

Understanding sound and specifically natural sounds, the National Park Service Government indicate that frequency is the number of waves that pass a given point in one second. God is always speaking; the question is, are we listening? There is always a frequency, a spiritual wave link, of sound proceeding from God that's being transferred down to the earth realm. The Bible declares that we are *seated in the Heavenly realms in Jesus* (Ephesians 2:6). However, again, the question is, are you in sync or in alignment with Heaven's frequencies? Are you connecting in the spiritual realm? For example, when your laptop charger is connected to your laptop, it is obtaining a current of electrical charge to give the device power so it can be operated or function effectively. Another example is when you plug your cell phone into the charger that is plugged into the electrical circuit outlet it is receiving an electrical charge to *reboot* the cell phone device so you can communicate, receive, send messages, and so forth. It is the same spiritual concept with us as humans. We must be spiritually plugged in to Heaven's current of power to communicate with God and receive messages, and power from God to function effectively. We must be connected to the lifeline source of who is God, the Creator of the Universe and all creation and living organisms. I often say, God is the very fiber of my being, who holds me together. God is the very source of my existence. Scientifically speaking, the National Institutes of Health, and National Library of Medicine indicates that the human body is made up of trillions of cells that are the basic unit of life, which perform various functions. The human body's cells are made up of atoms, which are molecules, a collection of atoms (NIH, NLM 2021). Wikipedia provides pertinent information about how atoms consist of a nucleus containing protons and neutrons, surrounded by electrons.

Therefore, humans are made up of cells rather than electrons. Our physical bodies have volume and mass that can be weighed and measured. Moreover, we are spirit beings, too. Our spirit is connected to God, the Creator, whom He, too, is Spirit. The Spirit occupies the human body but cannot be measured. Our Spirit is eternal and never dies. Therefore, just like lightning which is made up of electrons that cannot be measured, in the same way as matter or mass produces a current of power, and a surge of shock waves that illuminate the sky, God, too, illuminates our human *being* and existence. God, who is the source of all power, gives us supernatural power to function the way He functions while here on earth. That's why God says, in the Holy Bible, that we are *Ambassadors for Christ* and of the Kingdom of Heaven, sent into the world. We are in the earth to fulfill God's divine purpose powered by God!

According to Wikipedia, the mass of our human body is 99% made up of six elements: oxygen, carbon, hydrogen, nitrogen, calcium, and phosphorus, for us to survive and function in our physical. However, our spirit is the *"Breath of God."* Therefore, we need the *Ruach* (Hebrew word for Breath of God), His Spirit, to bring life to our physical bodies. The Spirit is what occupies the human body and commands every creative particle in the body to function as a living, breathing, and moving organism. In fact, when God created the first man, or human being, according to ***Genesis 2:7 (NKJV), "…the Lord God formed man of the dust of the ground, and breathed into his nostrils the breath of life: and man became a living being.***

"In the beginning God created the heavens and the earth. The earth was without form and void; and darkness was on the face of the deep. And the Spirit of God was hovering over the face of the waters." – Genesis 1:1-2, NKJV.

Again, God cannot be measured! God is infinite!

God is limitless! Therefore, time cannot be put on God. God is eternal, without end or beginning. That's why God says, ***"I am the Alpha and Omega, the Beginning and the End, says the Lord, "who is and who was and who is to come, the Almighty." – Revelation 1:8, NKJV).***

There was nothing before God.

Now, according to science, the brain, a living organism that is made up of matter functions on *Alpha* brain waves associated with relaxation, creativity, and a flow state of mind (Alpha Wave www. sciencedirect.com). The *Alpha* brain waves electrical activity can be measured on an EEG, electro-encephalogram, (Brain Waves – an overview, www. sciencedirect.com). The *Alpha* brain waves help minimize sensory inputs, clear the mind of unwanted thoughts, boost creativity, act as a natural anti-depressant by promoting the release of serotonin, and enhance the ability to absorb new information (www.calm.com). *Alpha* brain waves can be boosted by the consistent practice of meditation, mindfulness, deep breathing, and closed-eye visualization (www.calm.com). The practice of prayer, closing of the eyes, and taking deep breaths, relaxing the mind, listening to tranquil instrumental mediative prayer and worship music, focusing on biblical scripture and on God, engaging the five senses activate the *Alpha* brain waves.

I personally believe, when we practice these therapeutic strategies, we are connecting to the spiritual frequencies that come from God who is the *Alpha – the beginning of all things and creation,* and in the process, God is *rebooting* our cognition. As I said previously, God is the *lifeline*.

The Red Cross organization explains, when an emergency medical professional uses an AED device to resuscitate a person, they are reviving someone from unconsciousness or death sending shock waves by the way of a surge of electricity to the heart to reboot the rhythm of the heart to function again causing the body to live again. This is what God does! God specializes in reviving that which appears dead, with His resurrecting power. God sends spiritual shock waves of His power to put us in the rhythm that is in sync with Him and with Heaven. According to Wikipedia, rhythm is the repeated patterns of sounds, words, or movements, or a regular change in something. This is why music is so powerful. Worshiping God through hearing the rhythm of a pattern of sounds or beats, singing, dancing in movement, and in a spiritual posture of admonishment unto God is powerful! To worship God, is to show deep respect, devotion, and give adoration. Also, to worship God is to esteem God and acknowledge His awesome power, and sovereignty. We were created to worship God. In fact, worship is a lifestyle. A lifestyle of worship is walking in the rhythm of Heaven's frequencies, hearing what God is saying, living, and functioning in accordance with God's rhythm.

When I was in graduate school to obtain my Master of Arts Degree in Trauma Counseling and Crisis

Response, I remember partaking in empirical research studies. I learned how the practice of prayer, worship, and meditation affect the human brain in a healthy way. I've seen how studies have proven that various regions of the brain are activated and generate peace, calmness, happiness, and clear exceptional cognitive functioning. I've seen real brain scans, such as the functional magnetic resonance imaging (fMRI) photos which show how the human brain, and specific regions of the brain, were illuminated, highlighting increased, healthy electrical activity (Estes, Peyton, MS1, 2023). The brain regions that highlighted cognitive enhancement when a person is praying is the frontal lobe responsible for focused attention, emotion processing, emotion regulation, relaxation, cognitive processing, and social cognition (Estes, Peyton, MS1, 2023). Seeing this research study was quite fascinating, to say the least! I think about how God gives His sons and daughters, who have been adopted by faith through grace a heavenly language of prayer when communicating to God. This heavenly language is a sacred language flowing in the rhythm of Heaven. I can most certainly attest to when I am praying in my heavenly language of prayer to God, I feel strengthened, focused, calm, relaxed, at peace, and reassured. Following prayer, I can reason so much better. I usually have complete confidence, and clarity of the mind.

Language is a rhythm that operates on sound waves; *frequencies* (NIH, NLM, Fujii, S., Y. W. Catherine, 2024). Praying in your heavenly language in an unknown tongue or language that only God understands is lifegiving. Your heavenly language is a gift that God gives you. When praying in unknown tongues, it is a secret code between you and God. Not even the adversary of your soul understands what is being communicated between you and God. God responds to us as we pray in our heavenly language as we spiritually connect to the lifeline source of communicating with Him. When you are in spiritual rhythm with God supernatural things begin to happen, not only in your life but in the lives of others that may be connected to you. The Holy Bible says, in the book of Acts, that God baptizes us with His Holy Spirit to empower us for ministry, service, and confirms to us that we have His Spirit dwelling inside of us.

Praying in an unknown heavenly language, that is a pure tongue, is one indicator to confirm that the Holy Spirit is dwelling inside of you. Other indicators of having the Holy Spirit living with you is your transformed character that emulates Jesus, operating in the fruits of the Spirit (Galatians 5:22), and obedience to God. However, when God baptizes you in the Holy Spirit and gives you a heavenly language, it is a gift to edify you, and for His Spirit to make intercession of prayer through you (Romans 8:26). This intercession occurs based on when we do not know what we ought to pray for, the Holy Spirit makes intercession on behalf of us, situations, or for others needing divine intervention from God.

"Likewise, the Spirit also helps in our weaknesses. For we do not know what we should pray for as we ought, but the Spirit Himself makes intercession for us with groanings which cannot be uttered." – Romans 8:26, NKJV.

"He who speaks in a tongue edifies himself, but he who prophesies edifies the church." – 1 Corinthians 14:4, NKJV.

Furthermore, God teaches us in scripture that we are to *tarry* for the baptism of His Holy Spirit. ***"Behold, I send the Promise of My Father upon you; but tarry in the city of Jerusalem until you are endued with power from on high." – Luke 24:49, NKJV***.

Romans 8:9 (NKJV), makes it very plain that if you do not have the *Spirit of Christ,* you are not His. ***"But you are not in the flesh but in the Spirit, if indeed the Spirit of God dwells in you. Now if anyone does not have the Spirit of Christ, he is not His." – Romans 8:9, NKJV.***

Therefore, it is extremely pivotal to understand the power of the Holy Spirit, being filled with His Spirit and desiring the gift of the indwelling of His Holy Spirit. We must not frown upon receiving God's Holy Spirit and receiving the heavenly language that He gives us as a gift. Not only is this form of prayer vital to your spiritual wellness but it is essential to your brain health and physical wellness. Remember we are mind, body, soul, spirit.

Also, the Holy Bible teaches us that there is a *gift of public tongues* that operates in the gathering of believers or in a group setting, like during a Sunday morning church worship service, a corporate prayer service, etc. Then, there is the *gift of interpretation of tongues* that follows when the gift of speaking in tongues publicly is in operation (1 Corinthians 14:28). God demonstrates this to show that He is among us and demonstrates His power. The *gift of tongues* is a holy language, an untainted heavenly language on God's frequency in rhythm with God that is communication between God and the person communing with God. God is Holy; therefore, He speaks through a person who has been given the holy language that is the *gift of tongues* to speak directly to His people. God is giving a direct message to that group of people in association with His plan and purpose for those people at that specific time. Then, His message is interpreted in the common language of the people gathered by the *gift of interpretation of tongues*. I have witnessed this in operation of God's demonstration of power countless of times during church services. I have even operated in both mentioned gifts all for the edification of the people in attendance. It's quite remarkable to witness God's awesome power at work and even more remarkable to be used by God as a conductor of His frequencies for the spiritual electrical current to flow through!

Now, when I say *electrical current*, I mean it is exactly what I stated, "electrical!" To explain it best, it literally feels like a surge of electrical energy or waves of electricity flowing through my body and it's so powerful that my physical body feels like it cannot contain the weight and power of God's Glory! I often experience my body trembling or shaking, my knees buckling, feeling like at any given moment, I'm going to fall under the power of God. I have also experienced like waves of heat throughout my body. Jeremiah says it best, ***"...But His word was in my heart like a burning fire Shut up in my bones; I was weary of holding it back, And I could not," – Jeremiah 20:9, NKJV.***

There's no denying that God exists when you experience His extraordinary power like this. I also experience other supernatural sensations when in the presence and Glory of God. Sometimes, when I am praying, or praying for someone, or during worship, I feel as if I am spinning in an upward whirlwind, or funnel, for lack of better words. When experiencing this power, it's as if I am traveling upward to a different dimension! I now realize, that when I experience this, it's my spirit in sync with God's frequency and His surge of power.

As stated by Cleveland Clinic medical staff, humans are considered electrical beings because our bodies generate electricity through the complex of chemical reactions happening within our cells. The National Institute of Child Health and Human Development, and National Institute of Health states, our nervous system transmits signals through electrical impulses that are essential for making our bodies a network of electrical activity. The electrical nature of the human body is cellular activity which is when every cell produces electrical charge (https://health.howstuffworks.com, Layton, J., Mancini, M., 2022). Cleveland Clinic medical staff provides information explaining how nerve signals are when our nerves communicate by sending electrical impulses within their fibers: Muscle contractions; movement operating on electrical signals causing us to be moving beings. Finally, the National Heart, Lung, and Blood Institute informs us that the heart rhythm is also an electrical system that generates the heart to have regular heartbeats pumping blood throughout our body in the cardiovascular system to nourish the body, and to carry oxygen to the brain.

The human brain can be considered an electromagnetic field (www.sciencedirect.com, Ehshan Hosseini, 2021). The brains electromagnetic field is the electrical activity of neurons within the brain that generates a magnetic field that surrounds the brain (pmc.ncbi.nlm.nih.gov, Maclver, M.B., 2022). Medical experts of Mayo Clinic imply that brain functions primarily on electrical frequencies that can be measured with neurons communicating through rapid electrical impulses creating patterns of activity called "brain waves." We are influenced by this process of electrical activity to think and behave a certain way (www.bu.edu, Trafton, A., 2019). It is crucial that we tune into the right frequency. Moreover, it is extremely vital that we tune into God's frequency, hearing His voice, know God's voice, and obey His voice. Hebrews 3:15 (NIV) states, ***"As it is said, "Today, if you hear His voice, do not***

harden your hearts as in the rebellion."

I love what Jesus says in John 10:27 (NIV), ***"My sheep listen to my voice; I know them, and they follow me***."

Also, Jesus teaches us in Luke 8:11-12 that we are to make sure that we are hearing the voices of those who have been called, chosen, anointed, consecrated, gifted by God, and are subject to God. They instruct us according to the teachings of God as a guideline to how we are to live while on this earth. As I said previously, God's chosen people are speaking on behalf of God. God's anointed vessels or people, who He chooses to operate through are under the influence of the sevenfold *Spirit of God* which is the manifestation of the Holy Spirit.

As I mentioned previously, according to Revelation 4:5, lightning, thunder, voices proceed from God's throne, and the sevenfold manifestation of the *Spirit of God* are before God's throne found in Isaiah 11:2:

1. The Spirit of the Lord
2. The Spirit of Wisdom
3. The Spirit of Understanding
4. The Spirit of Counsel
5. The Spirit of Might
6. The Spirit of Knowledge
7. The Fear of the Lord

God commands us as James writes, ***"But be doers of the word, and not hearers only, deceiving yourselves," James 1:22, NKJV***. When we follow the *owner's manual* then we can operate and function the way we were created to function and move to our divine destination daily. It's just like when you purchase a new car. The new car comes with an *owner's manual* to give guidelines on how to operate all the features of the new car so you can operate the new car and move the vehicle around to get to your daily destinations. God is the "Owner" of our being. God created us. Therefore, for us to operate and function at optimal level in this lifetime on earth we must refer to the *Owner's Manual*, which is the Holy Bible, The Word of God which God inspired man by His Spirit to write, and the Word became the *Living Word* as Jesus fulfilled the Word and who is the Word. ***"In the beginning was the Word, and the word was with God, and the Word was God." – John 1:1, NKJV!***

God spoke this world into existence (Genesis 1). His spoken words as His Spirit hovered first over the face of the waters (Genesis 1:2) expanded in and explosive surge of electrical frequencies creating a shock wave of sound throughout the earth, establishing everything He created, including humans! Wow! Isn't that awesome! It gets even better, when He created humans, He created us in His image (Genesis 1:26). He created us to have dominion like Him and to be able to create and speak things into existence through the frequency of His spoken Word. Isaiah 55:11, states, that God's Word will never return to Him void but it will establish whatsoever He sent it forth to accomplish. You see, God's Word is ABSOLUTE! God's Word has already been proclaimed! God has set His precedent. All we must do as inhabitants of this earth that God created and better yet, as His sons and daughters, we are to operate like Him and decree His Word. "***So shall my word be that goes forth from my mouth; It shall not return to me void. But it shall accomplish what I please, And it shall prosper in the thing for which I sent it." – Isaiah 55:11, NKJV.***

We have been given authority as a "King's Kid" to decree a thing according to His Word and it will be established (Job 22:28-29). We are *kings* and *priests* through Jesus according to Revelation 1:6, meaning we reign with Jesus in Kingdom Authority! We are royalty! Know your identity in Christ Jesus and watch God reset your mind and renew you afresh! Spiritual awakening is what will happen. Spiritual Awakening is on God's agenda right now more than ever. In fact, that is why God instructed me to write this book. Too many people are lost, do not know their true identity, do not know the power that they have living on the inside that awaits to be activated, causing them to live powerless, and in a malfunction state of mind. God wants our minds renewed, strong, exuberant, healthy, and healed! We have the same power as our God to *speak those things that be not as though they were (*Romans 4:17). This was God's plan from the beginning before the fall of Adam. However, Jesus restored that dominion back to us! Hallelujah!

When we as believers in Christ practice scripture reading, meditation, worship, and prayer we are strengthened and renewed in our natural minds and in our physical bodies. When the spirit is generated on God's frequencies the brain is functioning at optimal level. As I said previously in this book, the mind, body, and spirit are interconnected. God is the God of *Restorative Health*! God restores mind, body, soul, and spirit. God *reboots* our brains!

When we make a cognizant decision with intentions to consistently focus on our spiritual values and engage ourselves spiritually to God's frequencies, we allow God to *reboot* our brains. As already mentioned, praying, praying in the spirit through your heavenly language or tongue, singing and dancing in worship unto God, as well as reading, studying, and meditating on biblical scriptures, heeding to God, and living accordingly with Jesus, something miraculously happens! Just as I stated at the very beginning of this chapter, *the human brain is hardwired for God*! Stewarding your spiritual health is just as important as stewarding your physical, and mental health. The spirit is the core of the human being. Therefore, you cannot neglect nurturing your spiritual health.

We are living creatures because the spirit has been placed in the human body by God. So, our physical body is only a shell or outer covering for our spirit which is eternal and is subject to an eternal home when we physically die on earth. This is why it is crucial that you know where you will spend eternity following death of your physical body. Something to ponder on and to take very seriously. Therefore, in saying this, we cannot neglect our spirit man. So, when we focus on our spiritual values, connecting to the true and living God the miraculous thing happens! We come alive, and God literally *reboots our brain*! It's been scientifically proven with efficacy that engaging in spiritual practices we increase the blood flow to our frontal lobes and to our anterior cingulate regions of our brain that enhance our emotional processes. Prayer is essential in experiencing the spiritual realm and keeping us connected to God. However, it literally rewires the brain. We become more empathetic thinkers, loving, happier, and peaceful in nature.

Frequencies affect the brain depending on what frequencies you choose to tune your mind to. Previously indicated in this chapter, recent studies have shown that sound frequencies do impact the brain directly that changes the mood, perception, and even physical health. Again, because our brains have been hardwired for God, this concept means that we are permanently connected to the circuits that cannot be altered. We are hardwired to be linked to the circuit pathway to receive power directly from God, as we connect to God. Just as a light bulb in a lamp is connected to an electrical circuit that loops through a wiring system that allows electricity or power to flow and perform a specific function to produce light that is how we are hardwired to God to function optimally. When we try to alter the circuit ourselves, by connecting to other sources to give us happiness, peace, gratification, etc. our brains go into a malfunction mode. God created our brains to function the way that He intended the brain to function and that is to stay in connection with Him doing what He commands us to do while living here on this earth.

Afterall, we are Spirit first just having a temporary human experience on earth according to the time allotted to us determined by God. God created the brain to tune into heaven's frequencies and not the frequencies of this fallen world. As the Word of God declares, we are in the world, but we are not of the world (John 17:16). We are to be Ambassadors of the Kingdom of Heaven sent to establish the Kingdom of God on earth as it is in Heaven (Matthew 6:10). Our brain is to be tuned in to the spiritual frequencies of Heaven, allowing our spirits to take the lead by living according to the Spirit of God, and not be led by our carnal or fleshly nature which is sinful.

According to the Word of God, we were born and shaped into iniquity and sin. Because of the fall of Adam that caused the world to become a fallen world, a sinful world, we are sinful in nature. So naturally speaking, our fleshly body is enmity to God. That's why we must be regenerated, born again, washed of sin, and renewed in our minds by repenting of our sinful nature, acknowledging our sin, asking for forgiveness. Next, we must receive the grace and mercy of God that was given to us during the crucifixion of Jesus, who was the ultimate human sacrificial lamb of God. We receive Jesus as Lord and Savior denying ourselves and our fleshly sinful desires to follow Jesus (Matthew 16:24).

Jesus is God, God, the Father is Spirit who came and manifested Himself in flesh as Jesus. God came as flesh through Jesus to lay down His life unto death to show us just how much He loved us that He was willing to redeem us! Jesus covered the sins of the world through atonement by the sacrificial blood He offered. The sacrificial blood was shed on Calvary to blot out our sins. We then are saved by His grace through faith (Ephesians 2:8) by receiving and believing in our hearts what God has done for us.

Then, we receive the indwelling of the Holy Spirit to be able to commune directly with God boldly and to help us live Holy; set apart from the world not gratifying the lusts of the flesh rather to please God in service unto Him. God commands for us to live holy. "***Because it is written, Be ye Holy; for I am holy." – 1 Peter 1:16, KJV.*** We are to renew our minds daily with the washing of His Word which is God's manual for a sound mind that resets our minds to think and function like He does! God *reboots the brain* when we choose to stay connected to the *eternal circuit*.

I want to shift gears here for a moment and talk about some common mental health related issues. When a person who is grieving, or suffering from depression, anxiety, post-traumatic stress, or other mental disorders the electrical frequencies are disrupted and changes the brains wiring as to how it fires off and signals the human body. Now, as you know as a human being we have real life struggles, life blows, or life curves that are very distressing and will cause us to have real valid emotional reactions. However, it becomes a problem for the emotional electrical activity in the brain when we allow those emotions to linger, or they are persistent. The National Center for Biotechnology Information, National Library of Medicine, and National Institute of Health reports persistent depression, anxiety, post-traumatic stress, and complicated grief without being processed; talked openly about and regulating emotions will cause the brain to rewire itself and interfere with healthy brain chemicals to produce causing a psycho-neuro-biological imbalance in the physical body.

When there is an imbalance in the cognition this may require a *reboot* or reset in the brain that could come through counseling/psychotherapy. Also, the practice of prayer to the Creator, God, Jesus, worshipping; singing, dancing, and clapping unto God giving Him all the adoration and praise connects you to sound waves; frequencies that are nurturing to the brain wave activity. In such, causing a process of rewiring of the brain promoting a sense of calmness, tranquility, and peace. This is why God tells us in Psalms 46:10 to "Be still and know that I am God." Often, you just need to silence the noise of anxiety, excessive worry, stress, intrusive thoughts and learn to shift your mind to Heaven's frequency, tune in to God and receive the flow of God's power that sustains you, strengthens you, and stabilizes you when the human body is in emotional, psychological, and physical distress.

A therapeutic cognitive coping strategy that I engage my clients in, is the practice of releasing stress by grounding themself emotionally, psychologically, spiritually in the here and now, and in the present moment. Centering yourself in the moment when you are in distress is a very effective cognitive coping strategy that helps alleviate anxiety, excessive worry, fear, depression, etc. (Matthew Tull, PhD, 2024). Centering yourself can help you to let go of negative emotions that carry negative energy in your body. I encourage my clients to be cognizant to invite calmness and peace. I recommend clients to listen to instrumental prayer, worship, and meditation music. I encourage them to relax, sit still, close their eyes, listen attentively, letting go of thoughts, worries, fears, tension in their physical bodies etc. Next, I engage their senses in the moment to the frequencies of the sounds in the music. I'll advise them when practicing this strategy to gently ask themselves *what sensations am I feeling in my body*? *What sounds am I hearing precisely?* Perhaps, it could be the sound of a piano, violin, certain beats and rhythms, ocean waves, the wind, along with the music, etc. This is a relaxation and mindfulness cognitive coping strategy that trains the brain to shift focus off the negative thoughts and toxic energy associated with the thoughts and feelings related to the distress that the person may be experiencing. This relaxation and mindfulness cognitive coping strategy causes the rhythm of the brain waves to come to a calm, tranquil, and peaceful state.

Centering and grounding yourself means finding a state of balance, emotional and spiritual equilibrium. The goal and focus are to promote a healthy mental and physical state of mind. When you are centered you feel calm and in control of your emotions. When you are not psychologically and spiritually centered you might feel lost or disconnected from yourself. Other benefits of centering and grounding yourself is a self-esteem boost, eliminating power from outside factors or concerns, external stressors that contribute to internal stressors, and negative thoughts. Centering and grounding techniques can help stabilize the mind and cause you to accept the good and the bad in life. A calm and stabilized mind can realize, understand that situations are always changing, and it is a natural part of this life. This life is not certain nor is it constant or remains the same. However, when we ground ourselves spiritually and center ourselves in God, we understand that God is constant, certain, steadfast, and remains the same. God doesn't change. With this understanding that God is constant and remains the same always, God becomes your anchor and stability to endure difficulties and hardship in this life.

Healthy ways to center yourself is to practice meditation. The Bible talks about meditation in many places in the book of Psalms and throughout the New Testament. Reflecting on God's Word and learn to apply the scriptures to your life is a form of meditation. Nurturing your spiritual relationship with God by talking to Him every day and including Him into your everyday life and tasks is a form of meditation because your mind is fixed on Him. The Bible proclaims, God will keep us in perfect peace whose mind is fixed on Him. ***"You will keep him in perfect peace all who trust in you, all whose thoughts are fixed on you." – Isaiah 26:3, NLT.***

Approaching meditation with expectancy, trusting God in total confidence and trust that He will speak to you through scripture or even through others and in other innovative ways is a very important aspect to practicing this cognitive coping strategy. Focusing your whole mind on the ways of God, Word of God, and His promises is another form of meditation. Doing breath-work when sitting in silence, stillness, and relaxing or while you are listening to instrumental prayer, worship, and meditative music is another way to center yourself. Also, I tell my clients God gifted us with an imagination, why not use it to engage in visualization.

Imagine things like a visual description of Heaven, God, Jesus sitting with you or holding your hand, etc. or imagining a tranquil place that is soothing, comforting, and nurturing for your emotional, mental, and spiritual health, enhances healing. Relaxation of your body, such as positioning yourself when meditating or stretching your physical body is essential in centering and grounding yourself, because you are moving and releasing negative energy throughout your body. This relaxation process enhances, regulates the various body systems to function effectively, and regulates the mind, and helps you to tune in your brain activity to God's circuit to receive the current of tranquility, peace, hope, love, faith, and life.

Another form of meditation that I practice personally and encourage my clients to practice is morning meditation prayer nature walks. It's my time to converse with God, listen to instrumental prayer and meditation music tuning in to God's frequency, connecting with God in nature and with His creation. This practice is a good way to reboot the mind, soul, spirit, and the body. The purpose is to be present in the moment, in the here and now, relinquishing my mind, shifting my focus on "The Now" enjoying the moment, and paying attention to how I am feeling in the moment. I am engaging my senses and grounding myself in the beauty of my surrounding, finding the good, embracing inner peace, happiness, and tranquility.

This my friend is LIVING! God tells us to be *anxious for nothing, do not worry, fear not, and do not be discouraged or dismayed.* It is so important that you do not miss the blessing in the "NOW." My mantra is *time is of the essence and time is one thing that you cannot get back.* Therefore, it is crucial that you embrace every moment in this life and do not take time for granted. It is important that you take every moment seriously and make the best of each moment given to you. Time is a gift from God and should be stewarded well. God wants us to prioritize and practice balanced living. God wants us to maximize our time to nurture spiritual health, physical health, mental, and emotional health.

There are major benefits when practicing mindful walking meditation that include:

1. Improving blood circulation and blood sugars
2. Reduces anxiety
3. Helps fight against depression.
4. Improves well-being.
5. Improves sleep quality.

I encourage you if you are not already practicing *mindful walking meditation* to prioritize walking outside 3 miles a day 5 days a week or at least 30 minutes 3-5 days per week. Listen to heavenly sounding instrumental prayer, worship, and prayer music on your earphones or simply listen to nature as you walk in a quiet tranquil area outside. Engage your senses; sight, smell, hearing, and feeling. The goal is to empty your mind, shift your focus and attention to what you see, hear, smell, and feel while you are walking that is pleasant and calming. Often, what you will discover as you connect with nature, you connect with God because God is intertwined with His creation.

God is in nature because He created it! When you are connected to God while practicing *nature mindful walking meditation*, talk to Him, pray, meditate on scripture, and allow yourself to do some self-reflection allowing God to speak back to you and touch you through His spiritual frequencies and heavenly current that is flowing from His throne into your space allowing God to occupy your whole being. I have discovered when I am practicing this form of meditation, I feel so recharged, and sets the whole tone for my day. I often feel energetic, rejuvenated, reassured, sharp in my thinking, have a clear mind, relaxed, calm, peaceful, balanced, and most importantly I feel healthy!

In Psalms 63:6 (KJV), David, the psalmist writes, ***"When I remember Thee on my bed, I meditate on the Thee in the night watches."***

Psalms 77:12 (KJV) states, "I will meditate on all Thy work, and muse on Thy deeds."

"I remember the days of old; I meditate on all Thy doings; I muse on the work of Thy doings; I muse on the work of Thy hands." – Psalms 143:5, KJV.

Meditation is a biblical principle. However, as mentioned earlier, it matters what frequency you are connected to when you are meditating. Taking the time to sit still in the presence of God, connecting to Him, communing with Him, and reflecting on His goodness as well what He has spoken in Biblical scripture is quality time well spent. Intimate time with God is a form of meditation that recharges the mind, soul, spirit, and the body. Therefore, I encourage you to make meditation and relaxation a priority and let God give you a *reboot.*

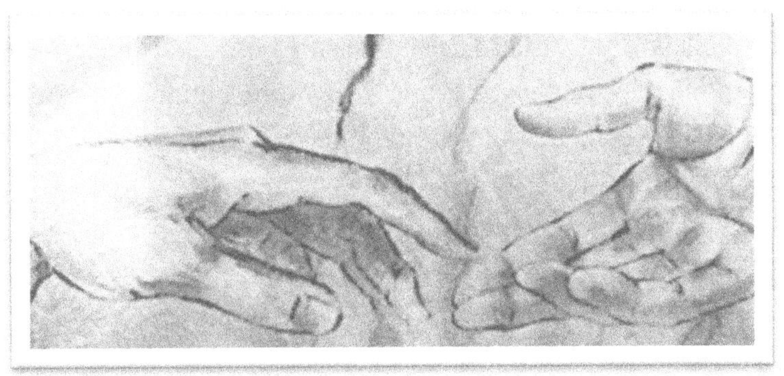

Chapter 8: God's Reformat and New Design

God is the God of the "New!" ***"Then He who sat on the throne said, "Behold, I make all things new." And he said unto me, Write: for these words are true and faithful." – Revelation 21:5, NKJV.***

These were the very words of God-Jesus who instructed the Apostle John to write this scripture as a precedent for many generations to come, even now! Jesus is telling you today, right now at this very moment as your reading this book, *behold I make ALL things new!* Jesus doesn't just make some things new but *ALL* things! So, think about when a computer is *reformatted*, the data or information on the hard drive is erased. A new set up of new information is replacing a new file system so the computer can be used more effectively. The purpose of *reformatting* a computer is to fix software issues, improve the function and resolve any problems. This is what Jesus, *The Wonderful Counselor* does. Jesus came to give us life and life more abundantly (John 10:10). Life is found in the one who is the *giver of life*. Therefore, it is up to you to tap into the source of life which comes only from Jesus who is our life sustainer and our anchor.

God is always on the move doing something new and creative! We simply just believe that He is. We must connect to the source of all power and receive what He has for us. The Word of God says that He doesn't withhold any good thing. All good and perfect gifts come from God. God is a gift giver who gives to those who are willing to receive. Your spiritual posture is important. You must demonstrate to God that you are willing to lay anything down that is contradictive to what God promises us that we already have. You must come to Him in your vulnerable state, in a spirit of humility, ask in faith, wait patiently, attentively, and in a spirit of expectancy. I may have written this already, but doesn't hurt to say it again, God is also a gentleman. God will not force anything that you do not want. You must consciously choose whether you want God to reformat you, your mind, and your life. You must choose to allow God to redesign a new you! ***"Behold, I will do a new thing, Now it shall spring forth; Shall you not know it? I will even make a road in the wilderness And rivers in the desert." – Isaiah 43:19, NKJV.***

You must recognize and know that God desires to

change the trajectory of your life and respond when the opportunity presents itself to you. What I mean about *respond when the opportunity presents itself* is, God is always watching. God knows the plan that He has for you. Therefore, God pursues you and there will be a divine appointment or time when God will reach out to you and want you to decide to get on the path that He has chosen for you. God's grace reaches high to those on the mountaintop and to those who are low in the valley. Jesus *came to save that which is lost* (Luke 10:10).

You determine the landscape in your mind by establishing new healthy and constructive neural pathways. These neural pathways are your thought patterns, habits of thinking, and core beliefs in your brain cognition. The landscape design that you choose will either change the trajectory of your life or it will keep you stuck on a path that God has not chosen for you. You must want change. Change just doesn't come. You must choose to change for change to occur as it relates to your mental health and spiritual health. Aligning yourself with God is crucial. When you are in alignment with God you can receive the spiritual frequency of change to begin the process of God *reformatting* your mind and your life. Your spiritual values and beliefs in connection to God's ways of doing things influence and impacts your mind that changes the course of your life for the better.

The human brain becomes comfortable with what it is familiar with or accustomed to. Our brain is conditioned and constructed to think a certain way causing systematic pathways that our brain wires itself to. This is why we must do exactly what the Word of God says to do, to *renew our minds* (Romans 12:2). The first step in renewing your mind is to acknowledge that the way you are thinking is not or has not been a healthy way of thinking. Next, you can confront the negative thought patterns. Finally, you are now able to overcome patterns of thinking that has created negative behavioral patterns that kept you stuck in a destructive cycle.

Identifying unhealthy thinking and changing the way you think based on what is true, factual, rational versus irrational, constructive, and healthy is the process of changing your negative thought patterns. I always ask a client whom I am working with on breaking unhealthy thought patterns that has led to mental disorders or unhealthy behavioral patterns, *to think thoughts that serve you and others well.* ***"...Fix your thoughts on what is true, and honorable, and right, and pure, and lovely, and admirable. Think about things that are excellent and worthy of praise." – Philippians 4:8, NKJV.*** I ask my clients to examine their thoughts, challenge their thoughts, and become inquisitive. I encourage my clients to challenge their thoughts by asking themselves, *are the thoughts that I am pondering on or thinking about true, constructive, is there any evidence for truth, and does it serve me or others well?* In this process of troubleshooting, I am teaching my clients to recognize how their thought patterns are irrational and could be cognitive distortions (Beck, 2020).

When Jesus engaged in dialogue with the many that

He encountered on earth during His ministry, He always challenged their thinking to help them open their mind up to something new. Jesus still does this today, especially during a counseling session when the counselor and psychotherapist is helping clients to combat negative and non-productive thought patterns to help clients reconstruct their cognition. This is why I absolutely love the human brain because it was created by God to reconstruct and rewire itself if the person takes the initiative to begin the process and is proactive in the process. Previously, I touched on cognitive distortions in a previous chapter. However, now I want to help you look deeper into cognitive distortions that have been extensively researched through efficacy. Cognitive distortions have been accepted in both clinical and non-clinical counseling practice and has received substantial empirical research validation.

As previously mentioned, a cognitive distortion is an inaccurate or biased thought pattern that causes a person to perceive reality in a distorted way. When a person has a distorted thinking pattern, this leads to negative emotions and behaviors associated with exaggerated or irrational interpretations of situations. Essentially, this thought process serves as a mental filter that can skew how someone views themselves and the world around them. I often say when counseling others, *if you can change your perception, control your mind by stewarding your thoughts well, you can change how you perceive the world around you for the better.* Rather than seeing people, situations, and the world through a distorted lens, viewing things distortedly and now have a false reality it is important to perceive through the lens of truth. When a person has a faulty mental filter, the distorted thoughts contribute to mental health conditions like anxiety and depression. Also, compulsions, obsessions, impulsivity, control, power, manipulative behaviors, and vindictive behaviors, etc. can stem from underlying patterns of distorted thinking that has conditioned the cognition to react or respond in these unhealthy behavioral patterns.

An example of someone who may exemplify these behaviors, is a person who has deep unhealed wounds of being rejected and felt powerless sometime throughout their human development. Perhaps, someone who has experienced emotional, mental, spiritual, and verbal abuse now becomes hurtful to others. This someone may have grown up in a home with Authoritarian Parenting Style demonstrated by a parent in the family system. The parent was rigid, absolute in their thinking, insensitive, non-empathetic, ruled with an iron fist, and oppressed that someone who once was a child now an adult leaving them feeling powerless. That grown up adult is now experiencing arrested development, still feeling powerless and hurting internally.

For these reasons, over time, the person may have developed a distorted thinking pattern and developed a distorted core belief. This distorted core belief could insinuate that everyone who does not provide validation, nor does not agree with them, or does not cooperate with them the way they want others to comply with them are perceived as a threat. Perhaps, when a person or people do not meet the unrealistic expectation of the one who has a distorted core belief is now perceiving that person or people as either "out to get them", is defiant, or perhaps spiritually speaking as we've heard it in the Christian faith, is a "Jezebel" rebellious, or defiant person. When the truth of the matter is an unhealed person who is a survivor of trauma of some type of abuse having felt powerless has now grown up and moved on throughout life still stuck in this developmental stage of their life. The unhealed person has the root of powerlessness, and now with this faulty mental filter, misperceives others and situations. This distorted mental filter is always leading the person to point the blame on others and find fault with others which is blame-shifting. The distorted mental filter causes the unhealed person to imply that others are in the wrong when it's the unrealistic perception of the unhealed person with distorted thought patterns.

Often, a person with patterns of distorted cognitions has communication barriers, interpersonal communication issues, and interactive social deficits that lead to having misconstrued information. Also, a person with cognitive distortions often misinterprets others or have a misperception about others and situations. People with cognitive distortions are poor problem solvers, very critical of others, and lack healthy conflict resolution skills. What's even more detrimental that I have witnessed as a Qualified Mental Health Professional, is often people with prolonged patterns of cognitive distortions suffer from mental disorders such as *antisocial personality and narcissistic personality disorders* (DSM-5-TR). These personality disorders exemplify lack of empathy, insensitivity, disregard other people's feelings, lack of remorse, manipulative, hostile, love to feel important, have a sense of entitlement, and love to have control or power.

People with these mental disorders gravitate to positions of great power and influence. Because of this unhealed or unresolved mindset, it is gratifying for a person who has not healed from "powerlessness" because of some type of past trauma or negligence. It is gratifying for a person who has not been healed from deep unresolved feelings of powerlessness to exemplify power over others to feel a sense of security or of importance. I have witnessed this issue among executives, administrative leaders, and supervisors in the professional sector, institutions, workplaces, community organizations, and even in faith organizations within leadership roles, using power and influence in such to weaponize others. Religious trauma driven by power, manipulation, and control has certainly been prevalent in faith-based entities. However, Jesus hates this and forbids this type of behavior.

I believe that I am writing this book to allow the Holy Spirit to lead many into mental, emotional, and spiritual freedom from the power of darkness, and to be led into truth. Jesus doesn't want us in the dark about these mental health related issues. Jesus has delivered us from the power of darkness (Colossians 1:13). As an author, mental health professional, and God's instrument in His hand, I have come to shed light on these mental health issues that are often not understood, unidentified, looked over, ignored, and have been existing for a prolonged period in the lives of so many people that it has become the norm. As believers and followers of Jesus Christ, we certainly cannot be okay with these mental health issues in the Body of Christ.

We as the Body of Christ cannot be deceived. We cannot allow these mental health issues of distorted cognitive patterns that has caused so many issues in the lives of so many people and has been used as a divisive mechanism even among believers in Christ. Jesus is eradicating these mental health issues. Time is of the essence. Time is winding down as we look at the biblical prophetic time, we are currently living in. God, the Father is commissioning His sons and daughters to prepare the way for the coming of our Lord Jesus! God is preparing the *Bride of Christ*, the Church. God wants our minds renewed, hearts purified, our spirit strong, exuberant now more than ever, and ready to meet our Lord! God is a Holy God, and we too must be Holy, dismantling any dark, evil, and wicked way of thinking. As I mentioned before, God is Truth, and it is the truth that sets you free! As sons and daughters of God we are to walk in a spirit of truth.

The Word of God declares that we have the "Mind of Christ" (1 Corinthians 2:16). Well then, we must cultivate the carnal mind to attain what God said that we already have! You can't expect to have the *Mind of*

Christ if you are not yielded to Him, and the Holy Spirit who leads us into *ALL truth* (John 16:13). We are to do exactly what the Bible instructs us to do, which is to cast down vain imaginations, and every thought that exalts itself above the knowledge of God and the ways of God (2 Corinthians 10:5). We must bring every thought that is contradictive to God's ways and bring them in captivity and under the subjection and obedience of Jesus Christ (2 Corinthians 10:5).

We all have heard the cliché, that "hurting people hurt people." The Bible teaches us that it is the "small foxes that destroy the vine" (Song of Solomon 2:15). Jesus is the vine, and we are His branches (John 15:5). However, when you allow the small matters of your heart and mind to disrupt your walk with Jesus it *destroys* your connection, and relationship with Jesus, and you can't flourish and become conformed to His image and likeness. It is the Father's Will, that we walk and live as *joint heirs* with Jesus on this earth, free, victorious, and as a vessel of honor used for His Glory. I believe that it's time for many to heal mentally, spiritually, and emotionally. The time is now! You must learn how to acknowledge, identify, and then conquer the past hurts, offense, and hang-ups by giving them to Jesus so He can truly heal your heart, mind, soul, and spirit. You cannot overcome something that you have not acknowledged is an issue. It's time to take the masks off and stop walking around in a masquerade. God doesn't want you hiding behind religion going through the motions and ritual practices of faith. Nor does God want you to hide behind a title, a position of influence, power, or doing good works. God sees your heart and He knows the matters of your heart. God doesn't want you deceived and living as a lukewarm Christian. God wants you free!

Your mind is meant to steward thoughts and to steward them well. Mind management is vital to prospering mentally. If you want to attain good mental health, then you must take account of what you are allowing your mind to entertain. This is why cognitive processing therapy is so effective in counseling because you're allowing yourself to organize thoughts and put thoughts in healthy perspective. God does not want you to mask the hurts, the past traumas, and issues with a *form of Godliness,* and *denying the power* of Jesus that transforms you. Rather, God wants your whole mind, heart, soul, and spirit! Jesus wants His people to stop covering up the pain, trauma, misfortune, and hang-ups with religion, power, a title or position, or anything else.

God sees and knows all. He sees the deepest parts of us. Jesus, the Son of God in His humanity understands how the human heart can be so deceitful and full of wickedness and evil. Jesus wants to walk with you in this life with His *Spirit of Truth* that leads to true healing, victory, freedom, and inner peace. However, you must do your diligent duty to yield to Jesus. It is your responsibility to filter out any thoughts or ways of thinking that do not serve you well. Our job is to dispel any thought that is counterproductive to God's ways of thinking.

The Word of God instructs us to *guard your hearts because out the heart flows the issues of life* (Proverbs 4:23). When you do not guard the soul, which is your heart that harbors feelings associated with thoughts of your mind, you open the doors for deception, wickedness, and evil to come and lead you. This is why it is imperative that we do what the Bible teaches us to not let the heart lead you based on the harbored feelings of hurt, anger, bitterness, strife, malice, jealousy, envy, etc. Because the heart is flesh and full of deceit. ***"The heart is deceitful above all things, and desperately wicked; Who can know it?" – Jeremiah 17:9, NKJV***. Rather, walk in the Spirit and renew your minds with the reading and washing of the Word of God (Ephesians 5:26). Essentially, by the study and meditation of God's Word, the Holy Bible washes away negative or impure thinking and replaces these thoughts with truths and principles that are sound and constructive. Better yet, come to God with a spirit of humility as David did in Psalms 51:10, asking God to *Create within you a clean heart and renew within you a steadfast and right spirit.*

You must allow God to *reset* your mind. If you do your part and come to the Father, God in humility, acknowledging your wrong thinking, emptying your heart out to God of all the negative biases you will experience renewal in your mind. I am talking about the negative biases that cause you to focus on negative aspects of a situation or about others while minimizing positive ones. Also, negative biases and cognitive distortions that are not based on logic or facts rather assumptions or skewed interpretations is the very thing that Jesus is wanting you to let go of. Jesus wants you to break the pattern of these automatic thoughts. You must allow the Holy Spirit to lead you into truth and convict you. Then allow the Holy Spirit to teach you how to think in a healthy manner when those distorted thoughts occur quickly and unconsciously due to prolonged ingrained patterns of thinking.

God is a relational God, and He is big on relationships. Relationships are very important to Him. Relationships as to how we steward and invest in them here on earth is what is going to matter for eternity in Heaven. Often, when a person has patterns of cognitive distortions it is very difficult for that person to establish and maintain healthy relationships. People with misconstrued thought patterns disrupt the construction process of communication with others. Communication is what enhances closeness in a relationship, establishes trust, and builds a healthy relationship. As I mentioned before, having patterns of irrational distorted patterns of thinking cause unhealthy behavioral patterns of prejudgment, control, divisiveness, criticizing others, and simply mishandling people in your life. Relationship stewardship is imperative and truly matters to God. We will all be accountable to God as to how we treated others in this life on earth.

I would like to highlight some examples of cognitive distortions that I often point out when providing psychoeducation during a counseling/therapy session. As indicated, cognitive distortions can strain relationships, fuel anxiety, bring on excessive worry, fear/paranoia, suspicion, lead to anger, increase misery, lead to feelings of guilt, inadequacies, and frustration.

Cognitive Distortions: Beck, J.S. (2021), Cognitive Behavior Therapy: Basics and

Beyond (3rd ed.). The Gilford Press. Beck, A.T., (1963.). Burns, D. D., (1980).

1. Catastrophizing:
   Expecting the worst possible outcome in every situation

2. Overgeneralization:
   Making broad negative conclusions based on a single event

3. Labeling:
   Applying negative labels to oneself or others based on a single action

4. Mind reading:
   Assuming what others are thinking without evidence.

5. Discounting the positives:
   Minimizing positive experiences or achievements

6. All or Nothing Thinking:
   You see things in black and white with no room for

   Reasoning or reconsideration for your thoughts.

7. Emotional Reasoning:
   Assuming that your negative emotions and feelings

reflect the way things really are.

8. Mental Filter:

Pick out a single negative detail and dwell on it exclusively so that your vision of all reality become darkened.

9. Fortune Teller Error:

Anticipate that things will turn out badly and feel convinced that your prediction is an already established fact.

10. Jumping to Conclusions:

Make a negative interpretation even though there are no definite facts that support your conclusion.

11. Personalization:

See yourself as the cause of some negative external event that you were not primarily responsible for.

12. Should Statements:

Try to motivate yourself with "should" and "shouldn't", which are rigid and unrealistic self-imposed expectations.

I challenge you to learn, unlearn, and relearn as Jesus walks you through the process of reformatting your mind. Our brains are continually processing so much information. However, when you allow Jesus, *The Wonderful Counselor* to lead you in the garden of your mind, you will experience Jesus pointing to areas that need weeding out, and planting of new seeds. God, the Father who is *The Gardener* (John 15:1) will show you where the sun shines the most. Therefore, the sunlight can produce growth from the new seeds that are planted in your mind. God gives us water by the reading or hearing of His Word to nourish the soil where you have allowed Jesus to plant seeds of goodness. Now the soil is fertile, and the garden of your mind is now healthy.

Jesus will begin to establish the tranquil landscape of your mind and now you can walk through the garden of your mind in peace. The peace of God will rule your heart and your mind will be kept in perfect peace as your thoughts are fixed on Jesus. God transforms chaos in the mind into a garden. God creates a space in our minds and in our life for living things and no longer dead things. However, you must yield to Him and allow Him to do the work of redesigning you, your mind, behavior, and your life. God specializes in reviving and resurrecting things that are dead. Following Jesus' leadership, His ways of doing things, and thinking the way He does in every aspect of your life is what God has commanded.

We are created to follow Jesus. God has ordained for us to take the hand of Jesus and follow His leading. Denying yourself, letting go of what we think is right, and heeding to what Jesus says is right is extremely vital! Let this scripture and the words of Jesus resound in your mind right now, ***"Then He said to them all, "If anyone desires to come after Me, let him deny himself, and take up his cross daily, and follow Me," Luke 9:23, NKJV.*** In order for your mental health and life to reformat, you must take the steps of denying what you think is right.

The Bible indicates that the ways of man may seem

right to them in their own eyes, and plans his or her own way, but it is God that devises your path (Proverbs 21:2-3, Proverbs 16:9). You may ask, what does it mean to deny yourself? Denying yourself, means, to reject selfishness and worldly desires, to give up personal goals and ambitions that are self-absorbed. Letting go of resentment, unforgiveness, vengeance, and vindictiveness is denying self-absorbed motives surrendering all to Jesus and keeping your eyes on Jesus is all part of denying yourself. To deny yourself, also means to be willing to suffer or die for one's faith in Jesus.

As you deny yourself you conform to Jesus' example of living and are willing to lay down one's possessions or status. Not to negate your valid feelings as a human being in relation to human experiences but to not let the negative feelings dictate your life. No matter what you think, or feel is right may not be right to Jesus. Afterall, it is not about you, you are not your own. Everything in this world is about Jesus and the Kingdom of God. You belong to God, your Creator and placed in the earth to fulfill His purpose not your own. Jesus taught self-denial as a spiritual discipline that is essential to be called His true followers and disciples. When you understand this truth, you will begin to experience true transformation. Surrendering your will and hardships to the Father is to receive the exchange of peace of mind, joy, blessings, and a satisfying life.

John 10:10 (NLT) states, ***"The thief's purpose is to steal, and kill, and destroy. My purpose is to give them a rich and satisfying life." – John 10:10.***

I want to take a moment to pray for you right now:

Father, I pray now for the person reading this, Lord, lead your son and daughter into all truth right now in this very moment. Jesus, remove the scales from their eyes that have made them blind to what true life is. Lord, bring conviction right now by your Holy Spirit, and teach your son and daughter your ways. I pray now for a spirit of humility to come over you right now in Jesus Name. I decree, that you have a heart of surrender and repentance. Lord go into the areas of their minds and hearts where they have been stuck or conditioned to believe and accept that which is a lie. I declare Healing in your mind! I decree right now, that deception is losing its grip off your mind and heart. I decree now, the Spirit of Understanding, Wisdom, and Knowledge is bringing clarity to your mind. I decree now, that you are delivered from the power of darkness. I decree, your mind renewed, transformed, and your spirit to awaken now in Jesus' name! I declare that you are coming into the full knowledge of your new and true identity, and you are coming alive in the fullness of God and what He has created, called, and purposed for you on this earth in Jesus Name.

You are God's New Design, let Him continue to reformat your mind!

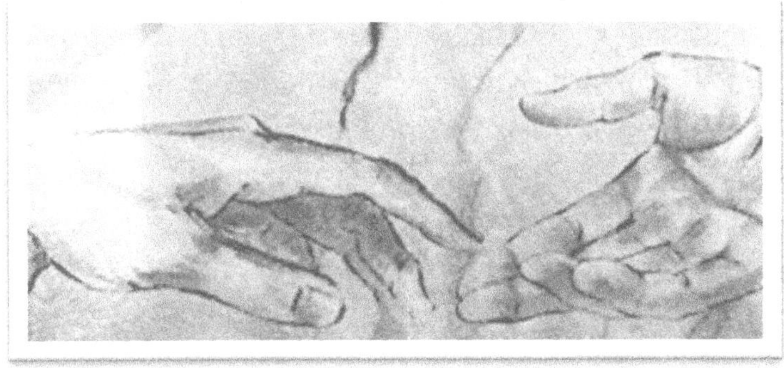

Chapter 9: Hope and Healing

"This hope we have as an anchor of the soul, both sure and steadfast, and which enters the Presence behind the veil." – Hebrews 6:19, NKJV.

Hope is the catalyst for change. Hope is a confident expectation in God and in His faithfulness that He will bring good into your life no matter what you are facing. To hope in God is to trust that God is good, powerful, more than able, and willing to do just what the Word of God proclaims in ***Ephesians 3:20, "Now to Him who is able to do exceedingly abundantly above all that we ask or think, according to the power that works in us" (NKJV).*** Let's be real, trauma, grief, tragedy, calamities, disparity, devastation and so forth causes us in our humanity to become hopeless, uncertain, and stunts our ability to continue in this life. I know, I've been there! If you haven't read my first book which is my memoir, *"Pain to Purpose", Counselor & Mom finds Hope and Purpose, The "Big 3" Revealed,* (Porter, T. 2024) I oblige you to read this book. I encourage you do so as it solidifies what I am claiming here.

I too understand what it means to be hopeless. As mentioned earlier in this book, when tragedy struck my life in 2018 facing the sudden tragic loss of my only son who was 20 years old and died in a horrific car accident, I was *stunted* if you will, for lack of better words. This traumatic event debilitated my ability to see hope in a murky, and unending reality of my son now gone from this earth and that I no longer would see him again. In an instance, just like that, here one day, and gone the next seemed so unreal. I realized very quick that dark dreary night that Jesus is certainly our *anchor* who gave me stability and something to hold me in place so that I wouldn't be swept away by traumatic grief and hopelessness.

As I talk about in my memoir, *Pain to Purpose* (Porter, T., 2024), hope penetrated darkness and my life that dreadful night when I encountered Jesus in the most tangible way. It was the night when I was in a state of hopelessness and heaven met earth in my car as I sat in the passenger of the car while my husband driving. Tear struck, looking out on the horizon of my car window as we were entering the city where my beloved son was killed after we had traveled for 6 long hours on the interstate, I saw Jesus! For just a moment, my spirit was lifted up in the spiritual realm where I saw Jesus walking towards me, and He looked at me with great empathy in His eyes sharing in my grief. Yet, He looked at me with such power and authority. Jesus spoke these words to me, *"Your son has risen with Me"* as the sun was coming up on the horizon in the earth realm as I was gazing out the window of my car. Then, I heard my son say to me, *"Mom I'm okay"* with such peace and calmness in His voice.

That was the pivotal moment that revolutionized me. I was instantly transformed from a state of hopelessness to now having hope. All the tormenting thoughts and voices in my head about my son's death in the tragic car accident ceased. A sudden peace and calm came over me and I knew from that point on that I was going to be okay and that my son is okay. Just as the Word of God states, *"death, where is your sting?"* (1 Corinthians 15:55-57) became reality to me. I faced the most difficult and horrific life tribulation known to humanity and as a parent, the loss of a child. This is a parent's worst nightmare to receive a phone call in the middle of the night indicating that your only son has been killed in a car accident.

However, God was right there with me during the tragedy. In our weakest moments and darkest moments, God is there, and He is near us when we are crushed in spirit (Psalms 34:18). God's grace is sufficient for us in the time of tragedy and suffering. God gives us exactly what we need in these moments of despair and hopelessness. God upholds us when what we suffer is too unbearable. Jesus comes to undergird us with His strength. ***"My grace is sufficient for you, for My strength is made perfect in weakness." – 2 Corinthians 12:9, NKJV.***

It is the natural human response to feel hopeless when you are struck with great suffering and loss. However, God responds and meets us there in the time of suffering. Healing comes when you believe this truth, open your mind and heart to receive Jesus, the *healer* and *comforter.* You may ask, *how do I do this*? Simply, trust in the Biblical hope who is Jesus our *eternal hope* who has paved the way for us all as the forerunner to endure suffering and gave us an end to suffering in eternity; heaven once and for all! Next, have an expectation, completely confident in what God promised us and not just wishing for something. Rather, knowing that you already have it in your possession as a gift given to us from the Father, God, our Creator.

Then, we embrace assurance which is having certainty in God and what He has promised us. I oblige you to think about when you have felt forsaken or let down by God, the God of love who loves you immensely and unconditionally. You may have asked *what do I do now when love hurts, and all hell has come against you?* I want to now take a moment and give you some strategy as to what you do. I call this *Heavens Pathway to Hope*:

1. You stand on the promises of God for they are

Yes and Amen! (2 Corinthians 1:20)

2. You put your total confidence and trust in the Father and believe what He has proclaimed, *"The battle doesn't belong to you, but it belongs to the Lord!"* (2 Chronicles 20:15)

3. Understand and know that the Lord has already gone before you and stands behind you as your *Rearguard* (Isaiah 52:12)

4. Look up! *Look towards the Hills which where your help comes from, Your help comes from the Lord*! (Psalms 121:1)

5. *Fight the good fight of faith* (1 Timothy 6:12)

6. You "***Trust in the Lord with all your heart, And lean not to your own understanding; but in all of your ways you acknowledge Him and He will direct your steps." – Proverbs 3:5-6, NKJV.***

7. Declare that ***"For God has not given you a spirit of fear but of power, and of love and of a sound mind." – 2 Timothy 1:7, NKJV.***

I preached a message *"Battle-Tested": When Love Hurts* at a church in Missouri just 2 weeks ago prior to me writing this. I talked about the content that I shared above, the 7 points of *Heavens Pathway to Hope.* It is imperative to understand that the testing of your faith is authorized by God. The testing of your faith is not to harm you or destroy you as I mentioned before. However, the testing is what makes you. The testing of your faith is what develops you. God is always in the business of conforming us to the likeness of His Son, Jesus. We are to emulate Jesus. However, we too must experience the suffering of our Lord, Jesus to identify with His character and understand how He walked through suffering. To share in Christ's suffering is to understand what it means to endure, persevere, press on, and then experience the Glory, triumphant victory that we have in Christ Jesus if we do not give up. That's the key principle right there, *not giving up*. Instead, we ***"…press towards the mark for the prize of the high calling of God in Christ Jesus," – Philippians 3:14, KJV***.

Jesus wants us to see situations in this life as He sees it. Jesus wants us to think as He thinks and possess His character. I love what James 1:2-4 (NKJV) states, ***"My brethren, count it all joy when you fall into various trials, knowing that the testing of your faith produces patience. But let patience have its perfect work, that you may be perfect and complete, lacking nothing."*** Patience is a virtue just as hope is. To be patient is to have the capacity to accept or tolerate trouble or suffering without getting bitter or angry. According to scripture in Galatians in the Holy Bible, *patience* is also a *fruit of the Holy Spirit*. ***"…the fruit of the Spirit is love, joy, peace, patience, kindness, goodness, faithfulness, gentleness, self-control; against such things there is no law." – Galatians 5:22-23, NKJV.***

Jesus knew although He was suffering greatly in His humanity while on earth, yet He knew that this life on earth is temporary, and He was not of this world. Rather, Jesus knew that He was of the Kingdom of God and Heaven. Jesus' hope was in the Father and Heaven. We too must understand this spiritual concept so we too can experience *hope and healing* while living on this earth. Jesus knew that God's love conquers all and God's love overcomes every time. Love wins every time! Jesus knew that God loved the world so much that He was willing to give of Himself as a sacrifice what Jesus became as God's only begotten son, Jesus *the Christ* to give others *eternal hope* in heaven.

I think about how I too, on September 29, 2018, had to give up my 20-year-old son to God who was His son first anyhow to experience the compassion that Jesus had for other parents who too would experience the loss of their son or daughter. Those who would be struck with the overwhelming pain and suffering of parental grief is who God divinely called and appointed me to. I was chosen by God to bring comfort and hope. God knew that I would develop the compassion to meet parents right where they are who would be hopeless just as I have personally experienced. I see how God used me as an instrument of hope to provide navigation for other grieving parents and pointing them all to Jesus our *eternal hope*. Releasing the pain, loss, anguish, anger, and the feeling God letting me down was the most difficult thing, yet the best thing I could have ever done. It was in this pivotal moment in my life when I experienced God's *perfect love*. For that reason, the torment and fear of traumatic grief and pain left me, left my mind, and soul. My life changed for the better. I felt victorious now rather than defeated. This is why the Holy Bible teaches us in 1 John 4:18 (NKJV), ***"There is no fear in love; but perfect love casts out fear, because fear involves torment. But he who fears has not been made perfect in love."***

I was being conformed to the likeness of Jesus in my experience of hopelessness, and suffering. I was now living out the Biblical scripture verse that states, ***"Greater love hath no one than this, that one should lay down his life for his friends." – John 15:13, NKJV.*** I had to understand the power of laying down my own life. Laying down what I believed how my life should be. I had to realize that my life is not my own. I don't get to have control over what God has given me. Rather, I had to understand, that my life totally belongs to God. Everything He has given me is a gift, and I am to steward the gifts God gives me. I had to be ready to release my son who was my gift back to the Father if He sees fit for the gift to return to Him. I had to let go of any bitterness, anger, and resentment as to what I thought I was entitled to have. As I have indicated, my son was Gods first, and I was not entitled to what I thought I would see him become, and everything that I still yet dreamed about for my son here on earth. I wanted to see him achieve goals in life. I had ambitions to see my son excel and succeed in life, and how I wanted his future to be. I had to realize that I was not entitled to keep him on this earth forever. I developed a mindset as Job did in the Holy Bible, when Job stated, ***"the LORD gave and the LORD has taken***

***away; Blessed be the name of the LORD." – Job 1:21, NKJV*.**

Jesus became our hope when He laid down His life for us so that we can have eternal life beyond the life that we have on earth. Jesus gave us hope. Jesus wants us to be *hope carriers* as sons and daughters of God. However, we too must be willing to walk through suffering here on this earth to experience becoming an instrument of hope. We must learn from our trials, tribulations, and testing of our faith. You must identify what you gained from the suffering and ask yourself, *what am I going to do with this suffering that I experienced or what I am currently experiencing?* Jesus endured His suffering, laid down His life to fulfill God, the Father's purpose on earth. We too must endure the suffering that we experience in our life and make a conscientious choice to fulfill God's purpose for our lives on this earth. I have done this and will continue to do this because, I now know my life is not my own. As a counselor, mom, pastor, author, publisher, and business owner, I have found hope and purpose. The story of my life is *Pain to Purpose.* Which is why I have written and published my first book, *Pain to Purpose.*

I know the battle of this life is downright difficult at times. Sometimes too difficult to bear. However, let me remind you my friend, you were given full armor for the spiritual battle to stand your ground. You were created for the battle! *"...Be strong in the Lord and in His mighty power..."* (Ephesians 6:10). I encourage you with the Word of God, according to Ephesians 6:13-17 to put on the Armor of God:

1. The Belt of Truth
2. The Breastplate of Righteousness
3. Your feet fitted with the Shoes of the Gospel of Peace
4. The Shield of Faith
5. The Helmet of Salvation
6. The Sword of the Spirit

What you suffer in this life is often the purpose that will come forth out of your pain. The weight of your trial is equal to the weight of your divine assignment and purpose. Losing a loved one to cancer or perhaps you had to endure a serious illness or may be suffering right now in your own body from a disease, God can use you to give hope to someone else in spite of what you are or have experienced. Moreover, maybe you are someone who has been severely injured in an accident and you now must live with the injuries. Yet, you gain a new perspective in your trial that gives you an opportunity to share hope with others.

When you experience Jesus in your valley, your low place of feeling forsaken, and you experience the hope Jesus gives you, now, you can share that hope with others. Who better can relate to someone who is experiencing a specific valley experience than a person who has already experienced that suffering. We are called and instructed by God to encourage each other in the Lord during our time here on earth. God knows His people need His grace and need to be reminded of His love. Therefore, God calls us to encourage each other daily until His Son, Jesus returns (Hebrews 3:13). When we share hope and encouragement with others, God's family is growing and growing strong. That's why the Word of God tells us to sharpen one another. ***"As iron sharpens iron, So one person sharpens another." – Proverbs 27:17, NKJV.***

God's plan and purpose is to always bring people into the full knowledge of who He is. God is the *God of Hope.* God is always thinking about souls coming into the Kingdom of God. God's agenda is expanding the Kingdom of God and making Heaven grow. That's why God charged man in the beginning in the book of Genesis in the Holy Bible to be *fruitful and multiply....and replenish the earth, and subdue it* (Genesis 1:28). God wants His children to walk in the fruits of the Holy Spirit and sow seeds of fruit in the earth to replenish the earth with more fruit and subdue this earth with good until Jesus returns, and we all receive our reward in Heaven. So, I challenge you no matter how difficult this life gets, choose to walk in the fruits of the Holy Spirit, *love, joy, peace, patience, kindness, goodness, faithfulness, gentleness, self-control* (Galatians 5:22-23). Our reward is the crown of life in Heaven and Eternity. Let us not lose sight of Jesus the *Hope of Glory*.

Jesus is the *Hope of Glory* living in the believer's hearts (Colossians 1:27). The hope we have in Jesus is living and active and gives us confidence in eternity.

This living hope is what God wants even the unbeliever to obtain. That's why it is crucial that we walk in *hope and healing* to bring this *hope and healing* to others all for the expansion of Heaven, God's eternal family, and all for His Glory. I want to be captured up in God's story who is the Author and Finisher of my faith, my entire life all for His glory! I often say, *my story is His story all for His glory!* This is the frame of mind that we ought to have as believers in Christ. If you are not a believer in Christ and as you are reading this book, I hope you have by now embraced the hope that we find in Jesus, and let it anchor you as you walk through this journey of life here on earth.

As I recently preached the message *"Battle-Tested"*, I stated, without *a battle there is no test, and without the testing of your faith there is no testimony! We are more than overcomers by the blood of the Lamb and by the Word of our Testimony* (Revelation 12:11). I have learned on my journey facing various trials and tribulations that to *lose is to gain.* I have learned, to suffer in pain, is to experience the glory that comes following the season of pain. In this life on earth, we go through suffering to glory. I want to give some scripture from the Holy Bible that solidifies what I am saying here:

1 Peter 4:13 (NKJV): ***"but rejoice to the extent that you partake of Christ's sufferings, that when His glory is revealed, you may also be glad with exceeding joy.***

Romans 8:17 (NKJV): ***"and if children, then heirs---heirs of God and joint heirs with Christ, if indeed, we***

suffer with Him, that we may also be glorified together.

Romans 8:18 (NKJV): ***"For I consider that the sufferings of this present time are not worthy to be compared with the glory which shall be revealed in us."***

Romans 8:19 (NKJV): ***"For the earnest expectation of the creation eagerly waits for the revealing of the sons (and daughters) of God (with emphasis).***

Romans 8:20: ***"For the creation was subjected to futility, not willingly, but because of Him who subjected it in hope.***

My mandate from God is to *Inspire Hope.* This is why I have been created, chosen, and called by God to write this book. Jesus has led me on a path throughout my journey in this life to bring comfort, love, peace, faith, and *hope* to the hopeless. God knew that there would be people right now in this period all over the world that would experience loss, pain, trauma, grief, tragedy, devastation, etc. God knew that no matter how much He has demonstrated His undeniable love for humanity, there were still going to be people who feel like they have been forsaken. This is when God uses people like me who have been destined to respond to the hurting as I too have experienced hurt. Also, to provide an answer to those who may ask, *what do I do now when love hurts?*

My response to you is to remember we *HOPE* in what we cannot see! However, we stand in faith, "***the***

substance of things hoped for, the evidence of things not seen." – Hebrews 11:1, NKJV. We put our hope, faith, and trust in the one who *perfects everything that concerns us* (Psalms 138:8). I challenge you to receive healing today if you haven't already. Let us hold fast to the truth that we are called to live on earth with *"Eternal Hope."* ***"But if we hope for what we do not see, we eagerly wait for it with perseverance." – Romans 8:25, NKJV.*** I charge you in the name of our Lord Jesus Christ to persevere, be persistent in faith, worshipping, and serving God despite life's difficulties and delay that you are facing. I urge you to never give up in the face of opposition! Previously stated, Jesus made a way for us as the *forerunner* (Hebrews 6:20) therefore we have *assurance* that everything is going to be okay. We have the victory and eternal hope regardless of what we suffer now and hereafter on this earth.

I remind you again of the words of Jesus in **John 16:33 (NKJV)**, ***"These things I have spoken to you, that in Me you may have peace, In this world you will have tribulation: but be of good cheer. I have overcome the world."*** I recite what I have written in my first published book, *"Pain to Purpose"* (Porter, T., 2024), *You are Spirit first* sent into the world to have a *human experience*! In other words, *an experience is temporary it will pass! That's why Jesus tells us, be of good cheer. I have overcome this world. There is purpose in your pain! God does not mean for your trial and tribulation to harm you or destroy you, but He authorizes the trial to develop you. What the enemy meant to use to destroy* *you with, God uses it for His Greater Purpose!* (Porter, T., 2024, Pain to Purpose). Also, I remind you of the reverberating essence of God's Word, ***"And we know that all things work together for good to those who are the called according to His purpose." – Romans 8:28, NKJV.***

You may feel defeated right now or have felt defeated by the circumstantial issues in your life. However, God's Word says to you now, ***"No weapon formed against you shall prosper, And every tongue which rises against you in judgement, you shall condemn. This is the heritage of the Lord." – Isaiah 54:17, NKJV.*** God foreknew you! He predestined you to be conformed to the likeness and image of Jesus. God not only called you, but He has justified you! Whom God has justified; He has also glorified! (Romans 8:29-30). So, to walk a life of hope and healing we receive, embrace, and live out God's everlasting love. Therefore, in the face of life's adversities, you can stand boldly and speak to the opposition and hardship in your life and say, *If God is for me, who can be against me* (Romans 8:31).

I want to encourage you to *not grow weary in well-doing* (Galatians 6:9-10). I encourage you to press on, and again I say to you, tell yourself ***"I press towards the goal for the prize for the upward call of God in Christ Jesus." – Philippians 3:14, NKJV.*** I remind you; *you will reap if you faint not* (Galatians 6:9). There is a blessing in your suffering. *There is beauty in every season, even the seasons of great suffering, if we choose to see it, and look for it. Your perception is your reality.*

Brokenness and beauty can co-exist if we choose to believe that they can. Eternal Hope and turning Pain to Purpose is my story all for His Glory! (Porter, T., 2024, Pain to Purpose).

Jesus is a master at taking our shattered pieces and putting it all back together to make a beautiful masterpiece. When we go through a season of brokenness, Jesus sees us as being *Beautifully Broken* (Porter, T., 2024, Pain to Purpose). I want this to resound in your spirit that what has been depicted throughout this book, *Jesus is your Healer.* Jesus will reveal to you that He endured the suffering and trials that you have or perhaps currently experiencing right now. In a season of suffering, you will experience Him more intimately. You will experience a deeper awareness of our Lord's presence. You will enjoy a greater sense of fellowship with Him because He understands and empathizes with you. Again, it's in the valley that you experience His tangible presence and comfort. As the psalmist, David declares, "***Yea, though I walk through the valley of the shadow of death, I will fear no evil; For You are with me; Your rod and Your staff they comfort me." – Psalms 23:4, NKJV.***

Sharing in Christ's suffering means to participate in the same trials and persecutions that Jesus endured. If we are created in *His image* (Genesis 1:27), have been conformed to His likeness, and are joint Heirs with Jesus, then we must believe that we too can endure when the Love we have in God sometimes hurts! We must love God so much---with all our heart, mind, strength, and soul. We must have confidence in the eternal love and bond that we have with Jesus, and that He will not leave us in despair or in a state of hopelessness. Suffering is a way to identify with Jesus and experience a deeper fellowship with Him.

Healing comes when we understand that according to Isaiah 53:3-5, Jesus shares in our grief; He is acquainted with grief; He borne our griefs. He was afflicted! He was chastised for our Peace, bruised for our iniquity, and by *His Stripes,* the slashes from the whipping that He endured on His back choosing to take upon himself for our healing. Believing in this Biblical truth will bring healing to you. True healing is believing in the promise and assurance we have in Jesus in eternity. Jesus is referred to the *"Man of Sorrows"* (Isaiah 53:3). Therefore, Jesus totally gets us. He knows and understands. So, let Him walk with you in the journey of life and in your valley seasons. We get the privilege of experiencing Christ in a tangible and intimate way when we are in a season of suffering (Porter, T., 2024, Pain to Purpose). Jesus relates to us in our suffering. It's there in the suffering, we experience His peace that overrides our understanding, and we experience His resurrecting power that restores the joy of our salvation! (Porter, T., 2024, Pain to Purpose).

To experience Jesus in this tangible way, we must do what David does in Psalms 51:10, Posture ourselves in a spirit of humility. Laying aside, our anger and bitterness, our will, what we think is right, give Him our sorrows and despair, and say, ***"God create within me a***

clean heart and renew a right spirit within me (NKJV)…. restore the joy of my salvation…, Psalms 51:12, NKJV). God is our *Safe Haven* (Psalms 43:2). God is our stronghold and our protection (Psalms 18:1-2). God is our *peace that surpasses all understanding* (Philippians 4:7). *God is the movement in your valley just as it is when a stream of water that flows through a valley between hills or mountains in the natural. It's the same spiritual concept, that when you feel as if your life has come to a stop Jesus being the living water flows through your valley experience and causes you to keep moving forward in life. Jesus is the river of life that nourishes your soul. Jesus makes sure that there is growth and causes us to bloom in the valley. Jesus is the "Lilly of the Valley" according to the Bible, symbolizing new life, resurrection, peace, and humility* (Porter, T., 2024, Pain to Purpose).

Just as the caterpillar goes into a *season of transformation* in the *cocoon experience,* we too are being transformed in the dark, isolated, season of change (Porter, T., 2024, Pain to Purpose). Something remarkable is happening! We are becoming something new in the transformation process. Therefore, we must *trust the process,* we *emerge* from the season of trials into a *new beginning of life.* (Porter, T., 2024, Pain to Purpose). As Job said it best, ***"Though, He slays me, yet will I trust Him…" – Job 13:15, NKJV.*** Job declared, Though, He slays me, yet will I *HOPE* in Him, signifying his unwavering faith in God even in the face of extreme suffering and potential death.

You must trust in God's goodness even in the immense hardship and challenges. Even if you face death, you must be so devoted to God that you will still believe and *Hope* in God NO MATTER WHAT! We are taught by Job in the Holy Bible to be relentless, unwavering in our faith, even when faced with difficult circumstances. I empower you to recognize who you are as a citizen of the Kingdom of God. You are a conqueror! So, I inspire you now to persevere and hold fast to what the Word of God tells us that, ***"The Kingdom of God suffers violence, but it's the violent that take it by force." – Matthew 11:12, NKJV.***

You may ask, *take what by force*? Take your faith and eternal hope by force not allowing the adversary of your soul to rob you of that what rightfully belongs to you! The enemy of your soul wants to rob you of your faith in God and your assurance of eternity in heaven. We must all be fully persuaded, never relenting in our faith and press on until we receive our *Crown* in *Heaven.* So right now, I encourage you with these words, embrace the love of the Father no matter how bad it hurts, and wait patiently for your salvation, the deliverance from your suffering. Let the *God of Hope and Healing* set you free from psychological, emotional, spiritual, and physical suffering. I beseech you now, to embrace *hope and healing*!

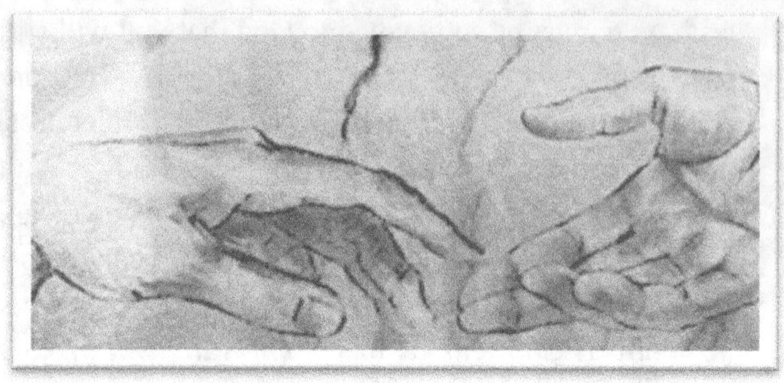

Chapter 10: Jesus, The Wonderful Counselor

"Come to Me, all you who labor and are heavy laden, and I will give you rest, Take my yoke upon you and learn from Me, for I am gentle, lowly in heart, and you will find rest for your souls." – Matthew 11:28-29, NKJV.

Jesus knows that in our frail humanity we can't maneuver this life in our earthen physical bodies without God's strength. We were not created to do this life on earth without the *Creator.* We were purposely created to function in God's strength, wisdom, and knowledge. Our lifeline and source is to be connected to the Father. When we try to do this life on our own, rely on our own intellect, and strength we grow weary. At this point life becomes too heavy to handle.

This life becomes laborious, and in our human frailty, we become overwhelmed, exhausted, weary and even feel defeated at times. The moment we refrain from coming to the source of our life we grow tired and even hopeless.

We are to lay down the heavy weight of this life at the feet of Jesus and take up His *yoke.* To take up His yoke means to submit to Jesus' teachings, authority, aligning ourselves with His way of living life here on earth. Essentially, we are to choose to follow Him and let Him guide our every decision and action. To follow Jesus' guidance is to understand that it will involve responsibility on your part but will also bring rest and peace because His *yoke* is easy, and His burden is light. Jesus commands us to come to Him with the real struggles of this life on earth and learn from Him. Jesus teaches us how to handle life issues with ease when we stay connected to Him. I have personally learned from experience to take the hand of Jesus and follow Him. When I did that, life began to be so much easier to navigate through. Once I began doing what I am instructing you to do in this book, Jesus proved to me that He handles this life way better than I ever could.

I have discovered, that when I come to Jesus with my life issues and lean into Him, I am empowered to walk through this life with wisdom, strength, peace, understanding, direction, and soundness of the mind. Submission to Jesus is to be totally surrendered, connected, and devoted to Him. When you choose to live according to His Will, putting your life under His leadership, He then becomes Lord over your life and not just Savior. Therefore, you are now in good hands, and you can trust in the one who will never fail you, abandon you, or harm you. God is faithful in all His ways. Even though you may not understand His ways as He instructed the prophet, Isaiah to write in the Holy Bible in the scripture, ***Isaiah 55:9 "For as the heavens are higher than earth, So are My ways higher than the earth, So are My ways higher than your ways, And my thoughts" (NKJV),*** we persist to trust His ways of doing things because He is the God of all knowing. God knows all and sees all. God sees the bigger picture! Trusting the process is so key when you do not understand what direction your life is going and why you must experience suffering. The process is God working on your behalf beyond your own understanding.

Finding rest in Jesus is the moment when you let go, give your burden to Him and follow His direction. You will experience that following Jesus is not heavy or oppressive, rather one of peace and fulfillment. We all must make ourselves available to Jesus daily. This entails, posturing yourself before Jesus to learn from Him, and incorporate His values into your life. You may ask, *how do I do that?* It's quite simple. Make it a priority to meet with him in prayer or time of communion when you are simply just talking to Him not just inwardly in your thoughts, but talk to Him out loud, then read scripture verses in the Holy Bible as the Holy Spirit leads you and make the scriptures applicable to your life. Study Jesus' character, actions, and ministry in the Gospels—*Matthew, Mark, Luke, John* of the Holy Bible the accounts of Jesus when He walked this earth over 2000 years ago and learn from His nature and do what He did. Allowing Jesus to live through you is the best decision any human being can make in this life.

Jesus, who became *The Living Word* is the light unto our path and the lamp unto our feet. Scripture states, ***"The word is a lamp unto my feet, and a light unto my path." – Psalms 119:105, NKJV.*** I urge you if you haven't yet or do not walk with Jesus to certainly make a conscientious choice to take His hand and follow His light that He gives us to walk through the journey of life here on earth. It is imperative to read the Holy Bible in its entirety to understand the fullness of God. Moreover, it's important to understand just how awesome Gods love is for us all when according to the Old Testament of the Bible mankind were once under the curse of the law because of sin. However, God always had a plan driven by His compassion and love for us to receive grace through Jesus and now we as mankind are *redeemed from the curse of the law* (Galatians 3:13-14), by the way of the sacrificial atonement of sin once and for all through Jesus.

Jesus Christ's act of becoming a curse on the cross of calvary for the sin of humanity is how you are justified by faith and believing that Jesus has done this for you. Now with that being said, let's dive into Jesus becoming your *Wonderful Counselor.*

Jesus gives us daily life principles such as:

1. Walk in Love

2. Walk in Light

3. Walk in Wisdom

4. Be Cleansed or Purified

So, we must be led daily not only by His love for us but reciprocate His love to others even when we do not feel it's worthwhile. Perhaps, you may feel that the other person or a group of people do not deserve love from you because of what they've done, said, or the toxicity they exemplify. Yet, according to Jesus, it is still very important to carry out love for others. Mental distress or disorders often are a response of not letting go and still harboring offense, hurt, anger, unforgiveness, resentment, bitterness, revenge, etc. Also, mental disorders are a response to not having a resolve regarding what a person endured. Trauma as discussed throughout previous chapters in this book is a good example of what I am explaining here.

When trauma comes into a person's life it is so deeply distressing to the point where the brain cannot cope with the traumatic event. God created us to have a natural psycho-physiological way to respond to high stressful events. This natural psycho-physiological response is the human stress response system. The human stress response system also known as the "fight or flight" response is a complex physiological reaction triggered by the body when it perceives a threat or a traumatic event. The human stress response system releases hormones like adrenaline and cortisol controlled by the hypothalamus-pituitary adrenal axis which prepares the human body to either confront the threat (fight) or escape from it (flight) by activating various bodily functions. Some of these bodily functions involve increased heart rate, muscle tension, and heightened alertness. Overtime, if a person does not process the traumatic event that was a threat or disruption of life, the human body does not return to a normal balanced state which may lead to post-traumatic stress disorder always in a "fight or flight" response state causing an imbalance of stress hormones and making it very difficult to manage stress.

People who find themselves in this psycho-physiological disordered state can become restless, angry, irritable, aggressive, on edge, tense, and on guard all the time. This can open doors for spiritual issues that prevent a person from *walking in love.* However, taking the initiative to be proactive in your mental, emotional, physical, and spiritual health is key. As I discussed previously in this book, Jesus is a *healer,* and He is the God of *restorative health.* Jesus does not limit himself to healing a person just one way. He heals in many fashions and as I indicated in previous chapters, Jesus is multidimensional, meaning He does things in a limitless manner.

Jesus is infinite in all His ways. So, when coming to Jesus and letting go, you must understand the infinite character of God. Therefore, it is not tabu to obtain medical and mental health treatment such as needed medications, supplements, and psychotherapy treatment to obtain healing. One thing about God is, He certainly has His people, His conduits positioned in the mental health and medical field who He operates through. It is important that you trust God that He will lead you to them. God doesn't want people to live in a disordered state. He wants you to *come to Him* so you can obtain rest for your soul.

Trauma is so complex and broad. As indicated previously, trauma can involve military combat, vehicle accidents, natural disasters, racism, terminal illness diagnosis, divorce, sudden loss of a loved one, bullying, etc. However, it is imperative that you understand that trauma can also entail all sorts of abuse such as: Being a victim of **parental abuse; Authoritarian Parenting style**, a parent who is rigid, insensitive, non-empathetic, non-compassionate, critical, may use religious/spiritual manipulation tactics to control and enforce obedience, controlling, manipulative, ridiculing, shaming, blaming, condemning, judging, etc. which are forms of emotional, verbal, mental, and can even escalade to physical abuse. **Sexual abuse**: molestation, incest, sexual assault, sexual harassment, sexual exploitation, martial sexual violence or abuse, etc. are other traumas of abuse. **Physical abuse** or **domestic violence** is a trauma of abuse that involves an intentional act causing injury or trauma to another person's body. Physical abuse is deliberate aggressive or violent behavior by one person toward another that results in bodily injury.

Spiritual and religious abuse are also other traumas of abuse that has occurred and may still occur in faith-based organizations, entities, and occults. I can confidently say that Jesus absolutely hates and forbids this type of abuse specifically because, as a result of the toxicity and abuse of the perpetrator, God has been misconstrued, misrepresented, and the toxic false distorted beliefs, actions, and toxic behaviors have been used to control, manipulate, and abuse, even unto death. Spiritual and Religious abuse is a deceptive, evil strategy, and tool to harm people. I have felt the spirit of God within me grieve when I watch something on TV about this form of abuse. I have felt God's anger within me when I witness it firsthand, or when I have responded to a victim and survivor of spiritual and religious trauma during counseling/therapy sessions. I have even seen when people take Holy Scriptures from the Holy Bible and twist its meaning to weaponize others.

I have seen occults and even occultic religious groups who take portions from the Holy Bible, twist or take out of content, add, and create their own doctrine or belief system to control and abuse others. Right now, as I am writing, I think about what God declares in the scripture verse, **Revelations 22:18**, ***"For I testify to everyone who hears the words of the prophecy of this book: If anyone adds to these things, God will add to him plagues that are written in this book." (NKJV).*** I share this scripture for you to be assured if you or anyone you know has experienced this type of trauma that the perpetrator who committed this abuse will be accountable to God and will eat the fruit from the seeds in which they have sown if they continue life without repenting and turning from this evil wickedness. ***"They***

will eat the fruit of their ways and be filled with the fruit of their schemes." – Proverbs 1:31, NIV.

I want to take a moment as I am being led to by the Holy Spirit to prophesy to you, the reader right now:

God is saying to you who have experienced any forms of the abuse I described above:

I know the pain that you have carried from the abuse. You were victimized based on

another person's bad choices and unruly behaviors. However, it is "I" who kept you

through it all. In this life, hurting people who have not surrendered their heart to me hurt

others. You were never at fault for any of the abuse. My Will is for you to attain hope,

healing, peace, and truth. Evil does not come from me. It was never my Will for you

to experience the evil inflicted on you by others choosing to do so. The abuse was never

a punishment for you and it was not a result of anything that you have done. I say to you

come to me and I will give you rest for your soul. I love you. The plans I have for

you is hope, a future, a good, and expected end. I know that you have suffered greatly.

However, after you have suffered awhile, I will establish you. I am the God of all grace.

I have called you to my eternal glory. I will restore, support, and strengthen you, and give

you a firm foundation. Let me heal you, comfort you, and console you now. You can't

change what has happened to you. However, you most certainly can heal and move on

in this life with my strength and with my help. I am asking you to let go of what

has oppressed you, give it to me, release the person who has hurt you, let me take it from

you and in exchange, I will give you peace, hope, and healing.

~ God

Your wound is certainly not your fault. However, your healing is your responsibility. I often talk about the power of forgiveness during counseling/therapy sessions when there is a need to discuss with individuals who are seeking emotional, psychological, and even spiritual healing often associated with some sort of trauma. The trauma is commonly associated with being victimized or abused by someone. I tell my clients; *forgiveness is not necessarily for the person who hurt you. Rather, forgiveness is for you, to free yourself from any negative emotional or psychological ties of oppression associated with that person.* An apology is something you may not always receive from the person or people who hurt you or who may have caused trauma in your life. You must be okay with not obtaining an apology or remorse from people who caused pain in your life.

Accepting the reality that people are not always going to be apologetic is key in your psychological and emotional healing. God doesn't want what happened to you to become your identity in life. It is not God's Will for you to take on mental disorders as your identity. Instead, God wants you to take the initiative to do some self-inventory, explore what's happened to you, be inquisitive, and identify the hurts and traumas in your life. God wants you to confront the pain and trauma head on.

Acknowledging what's happened to you by giving yourself space and time to openly process and express the feelings that you may have suppressed or repressed is a key element in the healing process. I guarantee you that Jesus, *"The Wonderful Counselor"* will meet you there when you decide to take this first step on your healing journey. Talking about your trauma or past hurts with a trusted confidant, pastor/minister, and skilled counselor or mental health professional is extremely healthy, effective and constructive. When you process by telling your story you are allowing your brain to heal and desensitize. What once felt so enormous and too heavy to carry now becomes lighter. This is how you heal!

I mentioned earlier in the text of this book, God instructs us in scripture to share your burdens with one another so that you may be healed. Sharing the burdens or distress you have with a trusted person means to communicate your difficulties, problems, and emotional weight. This strategy allows other people to offer support, understanding, and help you carry the heavy load. Creating a sense of shared responsibility creates a stronger bond, community, and relationships. Empathy and validation are one of the greatest healing components in such it allows you to feel valued.

As I indicated previously, when a person feels heard and understood, they feel respected valued, and loved. In the process of receiving empathy and validation the toxic residue of feeling invalidated, rejected, abandoned, betrayed, devalued, and unloved, is now restoring what was disrupted in your life and development. Sharing emotional vulnerabilities can deepen relationships and foster trust. Trust is often the first thing that goes out the window when a person or people who may have failed you, violated you, hurt you, and caused trauma in your life. Trust that has been sabotaged by a person or people has even been a leading factor for not being able to embrace the love of the Father, God and trust in Him. This has been a reoccurring spiritual issue for many who I have served in my counseling practice for years.

Trust is the developmental building block for security. When trust is disrupted in the early developmental stages of life in the human life span development it causes insecurities and needs that have not been fostered well leading to identity issues. Identity is developed in the adolescent developmental stage between 12-18 years of age following the early and middle childhood development stage between 0-11 years of age when a child forms a trust, bond, and then security. The child and adolescent begin to develop self-confidence and has a sense of stability or a solid foundation to explore the surrounding world without fear, and uncertainties. However, when this process of development doesn't occur there are voids, and unmet needs. The child and adolescent now move on throughout the next developmental stages of human life with deficits. Sometimes, these deficits are carried into adulthood. Other times these deficits can occur following adverse experiences or trauma as an adult as well.

These deficits can be social deficits which may involve not knowing how to interpersonally communicate with others to establish and maintain healthy relationships. Shattered sense of safety causes the inability to trust others when the trauma involved betrayal or abandonment by someone who should have provided care and safety. Trauma survivors often experience hypervigilance and being on guard due to shattered trust that lead to a heightened awareness always on guard and scanning for potential threats even in a potential safe situation. Defensive communication can manifest or be a trauma response as a result of a hypervigilant state of mind preventing healthy relationships to be established. Fear of vulnerability in relationships due to associating intimacy and closeness with potential hurt or danger is a common social deficit that prevent trauma survivors to connect with others.

Social deficits hinder the formation of potential healthy relationships. Social deficits interfere with maintaining relationships due to fear and anxiety associated with trauma that can make a trauma survivor wary of new potential healthy connections or cause them to socially withdraw from existing connections. Social deficits related to trauma hinder interpersonal communication skills in the sense of not being able to share emotional vulnerabilities with others and have open and honest communication dialogues due to not being able to trust others.

Other deficits can involve, **language impairment**; communication, **cognitive impairment**; reasoning, learning, memory, and problem-solving. Deficits such as low self-worth or confidence, indecisiveness, lack of decision-making skills, and so forth can also occur. Behavioral deficits may involve poor social skills, emotional dysregulation, and maladaptive behaviors. These deficits can even occur when major traumas occur in any developmental stage of life, and leaving a person to relearn what was lost in relation to the severity of the trauma and the effects of the trauma on the brain.

Our brains are wired for safety and security. Therefore, if our brain does not feel safe or secure, the brain will drive the person to search for safety and security. This is how many people develop attachment issues, obsessions, compulsions, and have uncontrolled impulsivity that are major contributing factors for various mental disorders. Maladaptive behaviors such as hoarding, stealing for no reason, addictions, getting involved in unhealthy relationships just to feel safe and secure are associated with the major contributing factors mentioned above. People who suffer from major anxiety, excessive worry, fear/paranoia are occupied with rehearsed, intrusive, or repetitive thoughts about either the past or what will be in the future are behavioral deficits. Sometimes, people obsess with worrying about the future outcome or what will happen next in life.

However, Jesus, *"The Wonderful Counselor"* teaches us to not worry about tomorrow. ***"Therefore, do not worry about tomorrow, for tomorrow will bring its own worries. Today's trouble is enough for today." – Matthew 6:34, NLT.*** Jesus wants us to relearn what is constructive for us. However, we must be willing to unlearn what the brain has been taught. Learned behaviors that are toxic, non-constructive, and unhealthy must be uprooted to establish a new root system by the planting of the good seeds that Jesus gives us in the Word of God, the Holy Bible. For example, identity developed based on distorted or irrational thinking patterns, and false core beliefs about self, others, and your life can lead to a slow gradual process of self-destruction. What happened to you, what you have experienced, and what you have been falsely told who you are is not your identity. Your identity is found in Jesus. You were not meant to be conformed to the ways of this world. You were created in the image of God to be conformed to the likeness of Jesus.

Mental disorders are not to be a permanent label that determine your identity. They are indicators that require treatment, recovery, and healing. Reclaiming your identity is part of the healing process. Identity issues lead to attachment issues and co-dependency. People who struggle with not having a healthy identity are susceptible of forming unhealthy attachments and then normalize the attachment. This is where co-dependency comes into play in relationships. Co-dependency can be referred to as a relationship addiction that involves when one person believes that it is their responsibility to save the person. A Co-dependent relationship involves accommodating needs to build a sense of identity and sacrificing their role in the relationship. Co-dependency is when a person feels that they cannot live without the person who they have established an unhealthy attachment with. Co-dependent relationships involve not making decisions independently and feel as if one can't be apart from the other person in the relationship. A person who is in a co-dependent relationship involves when everything they do revolves around the other person in the co-dependent relationship. Co-dependency is the excessive emotional or psychological reliance on the partner in the relationship.

Displacing your reliance on another person rather than on God can become a form of idolatry according to the Holy Bible. God tells us that we are not to put our trust in *mere humans*. ***"Don't put your trust in mere humans. They are as frail as breath. What good are they?" – Isaiah 2:22, NLT.*** Idolatry is giving undue worship or reverence to someone or something other than God. When we put a person, a people, or something else before God as having first priority in our hearts it becomes idolatry. Placing more value or devotion on someone else or something else that which has always belonged to God is a form of worship. You see, we belong to God who created us, and He created us to worship Him and Him only. God will not share His glory with another god. When you make someone or something else as center of your life it becomes your god. Other examples in addition to co-dependent relationships that are considered idols today include, power, fame, money, self-centeredness, personal accolades and achievements, etc. The consequence of idolatry which is considered a major sin leads to spiritual separation from God and other horrible consequences.

"***For you shall worship no other god, for the Lord, whose name is Jealous, is a jealous God." – Exodus 34:14, NKJV.*** Now, even though God instructs us to not have jealousy in our hearts, this type of jealousy that God is described as having in the above scripture is the fact that, He will not occupy a person's heart in which He created with another god. God forbids idolatry in the hearts of man. God is either first in your heart or He is not your God. ***"No one can serve two masters. Either you will hate the one and love the other, or you will be devoted to the one and despise the other…" – Matthew 6:24, NIV.*** God requires exclusive devotion. The Word of God tells us that, ***"I know your works, that you are neither cold nor hot. I could wish you were cold or hot.***

So then, because you are lukewarm, and neither cold nor hot, I will vomit you out of My mouth." – Revelation 3:15-16, NKJV. Furthermore, David writes in **Psalms 146:3-4 (NIV)**, ***"Do not put your trust in princes, in human beings, who cannot save. When their spirit departs, they return to the ground; on that very day their plans come to nothing."***

Now that I talked about *walking in love* which is one of the principles that Jesus, *"The Wonderful Counselor"* gives us in The Word of God and how trauma can hinder you to walk in love. Trauma can cause you to be stagnant, stuck, and perhaps experience arrested development. Let's focus on the next principle that I highlighted earlier in this chapter, to *Walk in Light.* You may ask what does that look like to walk in light? To walk in light is to be doers of the Word of God always allowing the truth of God's Word to shine through you as a carrier of light to shed light on darkness, exposing evil, deception, and anything that is false and contrary to the statutes of God.

Walking in Wisdom is the third principle that I highlighted previously as a principle that Jesus gives us as to how we are to live as a son and daughter of God. We are not to live according to our own intellect. However, we are to live according to the direction God gives us. God gives us effective strategies to navigate through life. His wisdom is supernatural, absolute, sure and steadfast.

The wisdom of God is the divine perfect knowledge

and understanding to help you achieve the best outcomes and giving you great insight in all situations for His greater purpose that is beyond the human comprehension. The Bible tells us if anyone lacks wisdom that we are to ask for wisdom and when we ask, we must ask with expectation and in faith. ***"If any of you lack wisdom, you should ask God, who gives generously to all without finding fault, and it will be given to you." – James 1:5, NIV.*** The fear and admiration of God is the beginning of wisdom. According to **Proverbs 1:7 (NIV)**, ***"The fear of the LORD is the beginning of knowledge, but fools despise wisdom and instruction."*** Walking in wisdom is to live a life that is committed to God to obey His voice and Word always recognizing that God is watching and evaluating everything. To walk in wisdom is to always stay in tune with God, being attentive to what He is saying, doing, and making the effort to stop and think first seeking His direction before acting. I like to say to myself, *what would Jesus do right now in this situation?*

The fourth highlighted principle is to *Be Purified or Cleansed*. We are to allow the Word of God to wash our minds. Our way of thinking must be replaced with the thinking of Jesus. When we allow this process to happen, we are purified and cleansed. We must do away with every sin and weight that so easily besets us according to **Hebrews 12:1 (NIV)**, ***"Therefore, since we are surrounded by such a huge crowd of witnesses to the life of faith, let us strip off every weight that slows us down, especially the sin that so easily trips us up. And***

let us run with endurance the race God has set before us."

Jesus will soon come back for His bride, the Church, and when He does, He is coming back for a Church that has been perfected in Him and brought to a state of spiritual maturity ready for Heaven. ***"...That He might present her to Himself a glorious church, not having spot or wrinkle or any such thing, but that she should be holy and without blemish." – Ephesians 5:27, NKJV.*** It starts with us individually and then collectively because we are the church. So, we must personally strive to be more like Jesus every day allowing Him to perfect us in spiritual maturity. God is very family oriented and loves marriage and family because it emulates the church as His bride. This is why He tells us in **Ephesians 5:25-26 (NIV)**, ***"Husbands, love your wives, just as Christ loved the church and gave himself up for her to make her holy, cleansing her by the washing with water through the word."***

This leads me to talk about Marital Relationships and what is needed to have a healthy marital relationship to mirror the relationship that God has with the Church collectively and with us individually. We are the *Bride of Christ*. The greatest command that Jesus gives us all throughout the Bible is that we *"Love"* (Matthew 22:36-39). Jesus' response when He was asked, "***Teacher, which is the greatest commandment in the Law?" Jesus replied: "Love the Lord God with all your heart and with all your soul and with all your mind. This is the first and greatest commandment. And the second is like***

it: Love your neighbor as yourself." – Matthew 22:36-39, NIV. In **1 Corinthians 13:4-8**, God gives us the foundational model for how we are to love others, especially our spouses, and those in our family as well as the family of the church body in this scripture passage, ***"Love suffers long and is kind; love does not envy; love does not parade itself, is not puffed up; does not behave rudely, does not seek its own, is not provoked, thinks no evil; does not rejoice in iniquity, but rejoices in the truth; bears all things, endures all things. Love never fails*** **(THE CARE AND COUNSEL BIBLE, NKJV).**

Love is the bond that unifies relationships across the board. Love is clearly defined in 1 Corinthians 13:4-8. We must love God first and foremost wholeheartedly, receive His love for us and reciprocate this unconditional agape (pure, selfless, sacrificial) love to others. It is very difficult to love others if we do not love God nor is it possible to distribute that love to others when we haven't received the love God has for us individually. If you do not love yourself, it is evident that you haven't received the love of the Father, God. It is then impossible to *love your neighbor as yourself.* So, Jesus would tell you now, that you must get this down first to truly walk in the love that Jesus commands us to walk in. In fact, Jesus states, ***"A new command I give you: Love one another. As I have loved you, so you must love one another. By this everyone will know that you are my disciples, if you love one another." – John 13:34-35, NIV.***

Again, God is a relational God! God loves healthy relationships because He is all about building His

Kingdom family. Relationships is the most valuable thing that you can invest in on this earth. Relationships is the only thing that you can take to eternity when you leave this earth. We cannot lose focus on the most important principle and that is to love. Paul writes in 1 Corinthians 13:1-7 that spiritual gifts have no value if we do not walk in love.

According to 1 Corinthians 13:1-7, a counseling session with Jesus pertaining to relationships and marital relationships would entail: Love bears annoyance and inconveniences, not losing its temper. Rather, to be kind, considerate, and helpful. Jesus will tell you to rejoice when others succeed and do not envy. Jesus would gently tell you to not parade yourself, nor be puffed up in pride rather drawing people to the pure love that you are to exemplify. We are to emulate in a manner worthy of Christ. This manner is to be polite and not rude. Jesus will instruct you during a counseling session with Him to always seek to benefit others instead of seeking your own personal gain. Jesus' way of counseling is to inform people that you are allowed to have differences in opinions with others when discussing minor matters if you are not provoked to become angry. Jesus will challenge you to think no evil and make allowances for people's flaws. Jesus' method of counseling revolves from love and encourages others to not rejoice in iniquity, rather rejoice in the truth. Love believes, hopes for the best, endures and bears with one another. **(THE CARE AND COUNSEL BIBLE, NKJV).**

Healthy relationships consist of: **(thejenmoff.com)**

1. **Accountability**: admits mistakes for when wrong, accepts responsibility for behaviors, attitudes, and values.

2. **Safety**: Refusing to intimidate or manipulate, respecting physical space, and expressing self non-violently.

3. **Honesty**: Communicates openly and truthfully

4. **Support**: Support each other's choices, being understanding, offer encouragement, listening non-judgmentally, valuing opinions.

5. **Cooperation**: Asking not expecting, accepting change, making decisions together. Waiting to compromise. "Win win" resolutions to conflict.

6. **Trust**: Accepting each other's word. Giving the benefit of the doubt.

Communication is the building block for enhancing closeness in a relationship. Just as God commands us to commune with Him, we also have to make it a priority to value communication with others. How can a relationship flourish and grow if there is no communication? A relationship cannot grow without ongoing consistent constructive communication.

We must learn how to be present for others and provide empathy when needed to enhance healthy relationships. A healthy communication process in a relationship and especially in a marital relationship involves, what I call:

***"The 4 C's" Building Relationships 4 Christ*:**

1. Consideration

2. Cooperation

3. Collaboration

4. Compromise

I use this strategy in marital counseling sessions, and sometimes family counseling sessions to enhance constructive communication to improve relationships. *Consideration* is good practice when engaged in a communication dialogue with someone or with a group of people. It is imperative that you take the time to pause and learn the art of listening first before jumping to conclusions, making assumptions, prejudging, and interrupting someone in a conversation. Especially when in conflict, it is crucial to value what someone else is saying first before dominating the communication dialogue to get a point across. Remember, *love* is not self-centered, puffed up, rude, nor parades what you think is right or wrong. To be considerate is to simply be careful not to cause disruption or hurt to others.

Cooperation is also equally important to practice in a communication dialogue. The best way to diffuse conflict in a conversation is to understand the process of working together to accomplish a goal. *Collaboration* coincides with cooperation. *Collaboration* is the action of working together with someone as a team effort to produce change, resolve, or create a new perspective about a situation that is the subject of conversation.

Compromise is exceptionally vital when communicating with others because it is when you are in a posture of humility rather than prideful you are allowing for unity to come in and then mutual agreement can happen. Spiritually speaking, you are allowing the Holy Spirit to function, to lead into all truth, bring conviction, and teach what is the best resolution. Compromise allows you to bend a little and be flexible rather than control the conversation, nor be obsessive or possessive in a communication dialogue. We are to do what scripture says to do in **James 1:19 (NLT)**, ***"Understand this, my dear brothers and sisters: You must all be quick to listen, slow to speak, and slow to get angry."***

The Wonderful Counselor is our guide to all those who are willing to listen, learn, and heal. Jesus is gentle, loving, kind, patient, and gracious. There is no need to fear, doubt, or worry when coming to Jesus. He is slow to anger, merciful, and understands you better than you or anyone else understands you. Why? Because He is God! He is the Creator of the Universe and He created you whether you choose to believe that or not. Sooner or later, you will encounter God and you will have the opportunity to accept Him or reject Him. The choice is up to you. God is a gentleman; He will never force you to believe in Him or accept Him. God gives us all the freedom to choose. I hope by now after thoroughly reading the chapters of this book you can see clearly that God is a Healer! He is the God of *Hope a*nd *Restoration.*

You can't help what has happened to you and you certainly cannot change what's happened in the past. The past is the past. However, you most certainly can choose to forgive, heal, recover, reconcile, and be restored. God is in the business of giving hope. God leads us all with His gentle hand, and with His light on the path of becoming what we were created, purposed, and intended to be in this life. God predestined us to be carriers of light, hope, peace, and glory. We all have been given the freewill to choose the destiny that God has given us through Christ Jesus.

Healing and recovery are a choice. You must choose to act, heal, and recover. Moreover, you must believe that you can be healed and recover from all that has transpired in your life that has left you destitute. To believe is a powerful force and action that can catapult you forward in life. To believe is to simply have faith! I'm reminded of what the Word of God says, ***"What good is it, dear brothers and sisters, if you say you have faith but don't show it by your actions? Can that kind of faith save anyone? Suppose you see a brother or sister who has no food or clothing, and you say, "Good-bye and have a good day; stay warm and eat well"—but then you don't give that person any food or clothing. What good does that do? So, you see, faith by itself isn't enough. Unless it produces good deeds, it is dead and useless." – James 2:14-17, NLT.*** The Biblical meaning of faith is to be confident in what we hope for and assurance about what we cannot see, to trust in God and His promises, and believing what the Bible says about Him is true.

God sees all and knows all! God knows that trauma,

death, loss, grief, crisis, suffering, etc. are often inevitable and we are going to have these human experiences. God knows that trauma can be passed down in family. However, God also knows that healing can be passed down in families too. God knows that we will struggle in periods of our life, and He knows that the struggle is real. Yet, God also knows that He will be with each one of us through it all and He will never leave us nor forsake us. We on the other hand must accept, believe, and trust in this promise and have faith in God. Peace, rest for your soul, and soundness of the mind belongs to you! ***"The God of Peace will soon crush Satan under your feet. The grace of our Lord Jesus be with you." – Romans 16:20, NIV.*** God gave us the greatest miracle to obtain hope, healing and restoration! God is Jehovah Rapha, *Our Healer*! He gave us grace at the *Cross of Calvary* to hold us together and give us stability. Jesus with His compassion gives us counsel, peace, understanding, and guides His people with divine wisdom. Jesus shares in our humanity as *The Prince of Peace*, *Everlasting Father*, *Mighty God, The Way, The Truth and the Life*, and *The Wonderful Counselor*!

Appendix A: Do I Need Counseling or Psychotherapy?

(These are some indictors why you may need counseling or psychotherapy and not limited to other indicators that are not listed)

1. Restless; Unrest, psychological and emotional distress

2. Irregular sleep disturbances; change in sleep patterns

3. Feeling incredibly overwhelmed

4. Social withdrawn; avoiding social situations

5. Feeling hopeless

6. Inability to control emotions

7. Consumed with intrusive thoughts

8. Irritability

9. Just don't care about anything

10. Change in eating habits

11. Complicated grief

12. Relationship problems

13. Excessive worry

14. Anxiety on regular basis

15. Feeling depressed

16. Difficulty controlling anger

17. Poor concentration, focus, brain fog, memory loss, forgetfulness, trouble making decisions

18. Lack of motivation; Difficulty with completing tasks

19. Disinterest in enjoyable activities

20. Emotional Distress

21. Psychological Distress: inability to function at times

22. Feelings of low self-worth

23. Suicidal Ideations, plans, attempts

25. Self-harm behaviors

25. Obsessions

26. Compulsions

27. Co-dependency and attachment issues

28. Victimization

29. Addictions

30. Eating disorders

31. Self-destructive behaviors; unhealthy patterns & cycles

Trauma history or suffering from post-traumatic stress: hypersensitivity, hypervigilant, traumatic memories, flashbacks, disassociation, insomnia, intrusive thoughts, explosive anger outbursts, anxiety, fear/paranoia, etc.

Appendix B: Adverse Childhood Experiences

(ACE's occurred between the ages of 0-17 yrs. Old)

(Felitti, V.J., Anda, R.F., Nordenberg, D., Williamson, D.F., Spitz, A.M., Edwards, V., Koss, M.P., & Marks, J.S. (1998) and Anda, R.F., Fleisher, V.J., Edwards, V.J., Whitfield, C.L., Dube, S.R., Williamson, D.F. (2004)

Questionnaire for Adults: ***(Emphasis from the original ACE's Questionnaire)***

1. Have you ever experienced not having enough to eat, had to wear dirty clothes, or had no one to protect or take care of you?

2. Have you lost a parent per divorce, abandonment, death, or other reason?

3. Did you live in a home with someone who was depressed, mentally ill, or attempted suicide?

4. Did you live with someone who had a problem with drinking or using illicit drugs, including prescription drugs?

5. Have you ever experienced a parent or adult in your home ever hit, punch, beat, or threaten to harm each other?

6. Did you live with someone who went to jail or prison?

7. Have you ever experienced a parent or adult in your home swear at you, insult you, or put you down?

8. Have you experienced a parent or adult in your home hit you, kick, or physically hurt you in anyway?

9. Have you ever felt that no one in your family loved you or thought you were special?

10. Have you ever experienced unwanted sexual contact?

Do you believe that these traumatic adverse experiences have affected your mental, emotional, physical, and spiritual health? (***Traumatic events have been linked to mental health problems.)***

If you answered **"Yes"** to any of these number item questions and answered **"Yes"** if you believe that these adverse experiences have affected your mental, emotional, physical, and spiritual health, you may consider obtaining counseling and psychotherapy services.

Appendix C: Indicators of Common Mental Health Issues

(American Psychiatric Association. (2022). Diagnostic and statistical manual of mental disorders (5th ed., text rev.). American Psychiatric Publishing)

Anxiety, Excessive Worry, Fear/Paranoia:

Indicates that there are some prolonged internal stressors associated with unresolved or unprocessed trauma or complex crisis situations, past adverse experiences, and hardship. Indicates prolonged chronic stress.

Depression or other Mood Disorders:

Indicates persistent sadness, anxiety, or mood of feeling empty. Prolonged feelings of hopelessness, or worthlessness. Persistent excessive guilt or self-blame. Prolonged irritability, anger, or frustration. Prolonged loss of interest or pleasure in activities that were once enjoyed. These prolonged feelings may have been repressed or suppressed for a long period of time. When depressive feelings have been repressed for a long period of time the body stores these feelings and responds with physiological ailments. These physiological ailments could manifest as, unexplained aches and pains, headaches, cramps, digestive problems without a precise cause, unexplained physical problems, such as back pain, or migraines, etc.

Post-Traumatic Stress Disorder:

Indicates prolonged trauma or a series of complex

traumatic events that has occurred that was too difficult for the brain to cope with and needs medical treatment and psychotherapy to process the trauma effectively. Prolonged symptoms of hypersensitivity, agitation, irritability, hostility, hypervigilance, self-destructive behaviors, social isolation, flashbacks, severe fear, persistent intrusive thoughts, severe anxiety, or mistrust, guilt, loneliness, insomnia, nightmares, disrupted sleep patterns, etc.

Personality Disorders:

Persistent patterns of difficulty with relationships due to prolonged emotional instability. Prolonged developed patterns of impulsive behaviors, compulsive behaviors, struggle with the need to have control and power, and have a distorted sense of self that may interfere with significant problems in daily life. Prolonged distorted thinking of fear of abandonment. Prolonged emotional dysregulation of anger, anxiety, sadness that contribute to rapid mood swings and unpredictable moods. Developed a pattern and habit of distorted thinking and perception.

Appendix D: Nervous System Regulation

(Langley, et. al. 1900's)

Understanding The Nervous System:

Sympathetic Nervous System (SNS):

- Activates the natural human stress response- "Fight, Flight, Freeze" response.
- Responsible for increasing heart rate, respiratory breathing, and adrenaline levels

Parasympathetic Nervous System (PNS):

- Activates the state of being relaxed and is responsible for digestive response.
- Enhances relaxation, reduces heart rate, and helps you to conserve energy.

Signs of when you are experiencing dysregulation in your body:

(Porges, 2011, Porges, 2018; Porges's Polyvagal Theory)

- Rapid or increased heartrate
- Quick shallow breathing
- Muscle Tension
- Sweating profusely
- Feeling anxious, jittery, restless or on edge,

hypervigilant

- Fatigue
- Lack of energy
- Inability to concentrate or focus
- Feeling disconnected or emotionally numb

Helpful Regulation Techniques: (Porges, 2011, Porges, 2018; Porges's Polyvagal Theory)

- Short breathwork that requires you to inhale for 5 seconds, hold for 5 seconds, exhale for 5 seconds, hold for 5 seconds
- Deep breathing from your belly rather than from your chest
- Practice grounding techniques: Engage your five senses; Identify 5 things you can see, 4 things you can touch, 3 things you can hear, 2 things that you can smell, and 1 thing you can taste.
- Focus on your feet planted on the ground to bring your mind to a state of focus in the present moment and in the here and now.
- Muscle relaxation: tense and then release each muscle group throughout your body from toes and progressively moving up to your head
- To calm your nervous system; splash cold water

on your face, lay a cold wet cloth on your face, or hold an ice cube to activate the dive reflex

Strategies to Maintain Long-term Nervous System Regulation:

- Practice Mindfulness and Meditation: Present moment awareness to alleviate stress

- Physical activity: engage in exercise on a regular basis, go for walks, stretch, strength training, swimming, etc.

- Healthy Sleep Habits: 7-9 hours of sleep per night, create a bedtime routine such as use a lavender essential oil diffuser, use sleep aid lavender scented essential oils spray mists that you can spray on your pillows, drink a hot cup of herbal tea that helps you to relax and aids sleep, put away electronic devises at least an hour before going to bed, listen to white noise sounds such as ocean sounds, pray before going to bed, etc.

- Practice Healthy Eating Habits: Eat a balanced diet that is considered whole foods and superfoods, take all natural whole/super foods supplements, avoid large amounts of caffeine and sugar intake.

- Practice socialization: Engage in meaningful social activities, have regular healthy social interaction with loved ones, and practice open and honest communication and active listening.

Cognitive Coping Strategies:

- Challenge and reframe negative thoughts and cognitive distortions

- Steward your thoughts by managing the thoughts in your mind and analyze your thoughts to allow yourself to organize thoughts and place into a healthy perspective.

- Be compassionate with yourself, be kind to yourself, and give yourself grace, and understand that you are human, imperfect, and will make mistakes.

- Affirm yourself and use compassionate, constructive, and positive self-talk.

Sensory & Somatic Strategies:

- Use soothing and sensory items like a soft plush blanket that you can wrap yourself up with, use essential oils or other calming scents, and listen to gentle sounds in your space to calm your nervous system.

- Practice gentle exercises or movements to release stored tension and stress in your body.

- Carry items that help you feel grounded and calm such as essential oils, scented hand lotions, stress ball, fidget toy, have a piece of soft fabric with a comforting texture.

Self-Reflection Journaling:

- Track and write out your emotions, thoughts, triggers, and what helpful regulation techniques or strategies in your journal.

- Reflective questions to ask yourself: How am I feeling? Why am I feeling this way? What triggered me? What regulation techniques were effective? What can I do next time?

Obtain professional support counseling/therapy, or medical consultation when you need it

Endnotes

Come to Jesus All Who are Heavy Burdened and Find Rest!

1. Matthew 11:28

2. Isaiah 9:6 (New King James Version)

Introduction:

1. Beck, A. T. (1976). Cognitive therapy, and the emotional disorders. New American Library.

2. Felitti, V.J., Anda, R.F., Nordenberg, D., Williamson, D.F., Spitz, A.M., Edwards, V., Koss, M.P., & Marks, J.S. (1998) and Anda, R.F., Fleisher, V.J., Edwards, V.J., Whitfield, C.L., Dube, S.R., Williamson, D.F. (2004)

Chapter 1: The Spirit of Counsel

1. Isaiah 11:2 (New International Version)

2. John 3:17 (New King James Version)

3. John 12:47

4. John 3:16 (New International Version)

5. Revelation 4:5 (New King James Version)

6. Isaiah 11:2

7. Isaiah 66:1 (New King James Version)

8. Proverbs 4:7 (New King James Version)
9. Galatians 6:2 (New International Version)
10. 1 John 4:18 (New International Version)
11. Matthew 6:10
12. John 13:34-35
13. Matthew 22:37-39 (New International Version)
14. 1 Peter 4:8 (New International Version)
15. John 13:35
16. Genesis 1:27
17. John 10:9
18. John 14:6
19. Romans 8:29 (New King James Version)
20. James 1:22-25
21. 1 Corinthians 12:8-10
22. Romans 12:6-8
23. Ephesians 4:11
24. Philippians 4:8
25. 1 John 4:16 (New Living Translation)
26. Psalm 138:8 (Amplified Bible Classic Edition)
27. Proverbs 3:5-6
28. Genesis 1-3

29. Isaiah 9:6

30. Proverbs 11:14 (King James Version)

31. Hosea 4:6 (New King James Version)

32. Ephesians 4:23 (Amplified Bible Classic Edition)

33. Romans 12:2

34. 2 Timothy 2:15 (New International Version)

35. Isaiah 11:2

36. Genesis 3

37. John 15:5 (King James Version)

38. Romans 11:17

39. Psalm 3:3

Chapter 2: Mental Health as Your Soul Prospers

1. 3 John 1:2 (New King James Version)

2. James 1:17

3. James 1:17-18 (New King James Version)

4. 1 Thessalonians 5:5 (English Standard Version)

5. Ephesians 5:8 (New King James Version)

6. 1 Thessalonians 5:11

7. 1 Thessalonians 5:5 (New King James Version)

8. Beck, Judith S. 2020. Cognitive Behavior

Therapy. 3rd ed. London, England

9. Philippians 2:5 (New King James Version)
10. The Word Gives Us the mind of Christ (www.masters.edu), 2025
11. 1 Peter 1:16
12. Psalm 51:10
13. Jeremiah 17:9
14. John 16:33
15. Brier, J.N., Scott, C. Principles of Trauma Therapy A Guide To Symptoms, Evaluation, And Treatment (2nd ed.). (SAGE Publications, Inc., 2014).
16. Genesis 2:7
17. Isaiah 26:3 (New King James Version)
18. Romans 8:1-17 (New King James Version)
19. Romans 12:2 (New King James Version)
21. Ephesians 2:6
22. Hebrews 6:19-20 (New King James Version)
23. 2 Corinthians 5:7 (New King James Version)
24. American Psychiatric Association. (2022). Diagnostic and statistical manual of mental disorders (5th ed., text rev.). American Psychiatric Publishing

25. 2 Corinthians 10:5 (New King James Version)

26. James 1:7-8

27. (https://myclevelandclinic.org), March 14, 2022, Dana Foundation. Neurotransmitters (https://dana.org/article/neurtransmitters) Accessed 3/14/2022

28. 2 Corinthians 10:5

29. Isaiah 9:6

31. Matthew 26:41

Chapter 3: The Prophetic Counselor

1. Ephesians 4:11 (New King James Version)
2. Isaiah 11:2
3. Jeremiah 1:5 (New King James Version)
4. Goll, W. J., The Seer, The Prophetic Power Visions, Dreams, And Open Heavens, (Destiny Image Publisher, Inc, 2004).
5. 2 Chronicles 20:20 (New King James Version)
6. Proverbs 4:7 (New King James Version)
7. Proverbs 1:7 (New King James Version)
8. Proverbs 1:2-5 (New King James Version)
9. Galatians 5:22
10. John 10:11

11. Matthew 18:12

12. Dr. H. Norman Wright, The Complete Guide To Crisis and Trauma Counseling: What To Do and Say When It Matters Most! (Gospel Light Publications, 2011).

13. Brier, J.N., Scott, C. Principles of Trauma Therapy A Guide To Symptoms, Evaluation, And Treatment (2nd ed.). (SAGE Publications, Inc., 2014).

14. Lating, M. J., and Everly Jr., S., George. A Clinical Guide to the Treatment of the Human Stress Response (3rd ed.). (Springer New York, 2012).

15. American Psychological Association. Stress. (https://www.apa.org/topics/stress). Last updated 10/2022. Accessed 5/15/2024 (https://myclevelandclinic.org), May 15, 2024.

16. American Heart Association (https://www.heart.org/en/news/2020/02/04chronicstress-can-cause-heart-trouble)

17. Stress And Diabetes (https://www.diabetes.org.uk/living-with-diabetes/emotional-well-being/stress#)

18. National Library of Medicine National Center for Biotechnology Information, Stress and Obesity: Are There More Susceptible Individuals?

(https://pms.nci.nlm.nih.gov/articles/PMC59581561/ April 16, 2018

19. Stress and Cancer: Is there a Connection? June 6, 2024, By City of Hope (https://www.cancercenter.com/community/blog/2024/06/stress-and-cancer#)

20. National Library of Medicine National Center for Biotechnology Information, Influence of Stress and Depression on the Immune System in Patients Evaluated in Anti-aging Unit (https://pmc.ncbi.nlm.nih.gov/articles/PMC7417678/) August 4, 2020.

21. National Library of Medicine National Center for Biotechnology Information, Immunology of Stress: Review Article (https://pmc.ncbi.nlm.nih.gov/articles/PMC11546738/) October 25, 2024

22. Psalm 147:3

24. Isaiah 53:3

25. National Library of Medicine National Center for Biotechnology Information, Hematohidrosis – A Rare Clinical Phenomenon (https://pmc.ncbi.nlm.nih.gov/articles/PMC2810702/) July-September 2009

26. Luke 22:42 (New International Version)

27. Luke 12:48 (New King James Version)

28. Matthew 16:24

29. James 1:2-3 (New King James Version)

30. 2 Timothy 2:21

31. Isaiah 10:27

32. "The Blood Will Never Lose Its Power" (Civilla D. Martin, 1866-1948, and Walter Stillman Martin (1862-1912); Thurston Frazier, 1962, 1966- "It Will Never Lose It's Power", Andre Crouch, FRAZIER-CLEVLAND CO.).

33. Beck, J.S., Cognitive Behavior Therapy: Basics and Beyond (3rd ed.). (The Gilford Press, 2021). The Gilford Press. Beck, A.T., (1963.). Thinking and depression: I. Idiosyncratic content and cognitive distortions. Archives of General Psychiatry, 9(4), 324-333 Burns, D. D., (1980). Feeling Good: The New Mood Therapy. New York: Morrow

34. Revelations 12:11

35. Matthew 11:28

36. National Library of Medicine National Center for Biotechnology Information. Exercise Benefits Brain Function: The Monoamine Connection. (https://pmc.ncbi.nlm.nih.gov/articles/PMC4061837/) January 11, 2013

37. Matthew 19:26 (New International Version)

38. James 1:22

Chapter 4: The Great Physician

1. Psalm 107:20 (New King James Version)
2. Luke 5:31-32 (New King James Version)
3. Proverbs 2:6
4. Brier, J.N., Scott, C. Principles of Trauma Therapy A Guide To Symptoms, Evaluation, And Treatment (2nd ed.). (SAGE Publications, Inc., 2014).
5. John 9:6-25
6. John 8:22-26
7. Elements in Biological Matter (https://courses.lumenlearning/wmnmbiology1/Chapter/elements-in-biologival-matter/#)
8. https://en.m.wikipedia.org/wiki/kaolinite
9. National Library of Medicine National Center for Biotechnology Information. Manjul Tiwari, Science behind human saliva, (https://pmc.ncbi.nlm.nih.gov/articles/PMC3312700/#) January 2, 2011
10. Electrolytes, (https://myclevelandclinic.org/health/diagnostics/21790-electrolytes) American Board of Internal Medicine. ABIM Laboratory Test Reference Ranges-July 2021,

(https://www.abim.org/media/bfijryql/laboratory-reference-ranges.pdf). Accessed 10/6/2021

11. Oculomotor Nerve (CN III), (https://myclevelandclinic.org/health/body/21708-oculomotor-nerve), Last Reviewed on 3/1/2024

12. John 14:12 (New King James Version)

13. Mental Illness (https://www.mayoclinic.org/diseases-conditions/mental-illness/symtoms-causes/syc-20374968 , December 13, 2022

14. Psalm 34:17-18

15. James 4:14 (New King James Version)

16. Psalm 46:1 (New King James Version)

17. Psalm 34:17-19 (New King James Version)

18. 2 Corinthians 4:8-9 (New King James Version)

19. 2 Corinthians 4:10 (New International Version)

20. 2 Corinthians 4:8-9

21. Lating, M. J., and Everly Jr., S., George. A Clinical Guide to the Treatment of the Human Stress Response (3rd ed.). (Springer New York, 2012).

22. American Psychiatric Association. (2022). Diagnostic and statistical manual of mental disorders (5th ed., text rev.). American

Psychiatric Publishing

23. Walker, P. (2013). Complex PTSD: From Surviving to Thriving: A Guide and Map for Recovering from Childhood Trauma.
24. Van Der Kolk, B.A. (2014). The body keeps the score: Brain, mind, and body in the healing of trauma. Viking.
25. Courtois, C. A. (2014). It's Not You. It's What Happened to You.
26. 2 Timothy 1:7 (New King James Version)
27. 1 John 4:18 (New King James Version)
28. 1 John 4:18
29. 1 Corinthians 14:33 (New Kings James Version)
30. Psalm 68:19 (New King James Version)
31. Psalm 3:3
32. Psalm 121:1
33. Philippians 4:6 (New King James Version)
34. Proverbs 11:14
35. Isaiah 9:6

Chapter 5: The Prince of Peace

1. John 14:27 (New King James Version)
2. Precept Austin Jehovah Shalom: Lord is Peace,

May 31, 2024 (https://www.preceptaustin.org/jehovah_shalom_the_lord_is peace#)

3. Proverbs 3:6
4. 1 Corinthians 2:16
5. Romans 8:1
6. Overcoming Comparison: Reclaiming Your Energy, Jessica Cabeen (https://www.jessicacabeen.com/overcoming-comparison-reclaiming-your-energy-and-focus) March 22, 2025
7. Deuteronomy 31:6
8. Psalms 46:10 (New King James Version)
9. Psalms 34:15 (New King James Version)
10. Matthew 6:33 (King James Version)
11. John 14:15
12. Matthew 6:34
13. Healthy Lifestyle Consumer Health Mindful Exercises (https://www.mayoclinic.org/healthy-lifestyle/consumer-health/in-depth/minduflness-exercises/art-20046356), Mayo Clinic Staff, October 11, 2022
14. Matthew 5:9 (New King James Version)
15. Proverbs 16:7 (New King James Version)

16. Psalms 4:8

17. National Library of Medicine National Center for Biotechnology Information (https://www.ncbi.nlm.nih.gov/books/NBK482512#) Physiology of Sleep, Joshua E. Brinkman Vamsi Reddy; Sandeep Sharmar, Last Update: April 3, 2023

18. Proverbs 3:24 (New King James Version)

19. Song of Solomon 2:1

20. Isaiah 26:3-4

Chapter 6: A Sound Mind

1. Philippians 2:5 (New King James Version)

2. National Library of Medicine National Center for Biotechnology Information (https://pmc.ncbi.nlm.nih.gov/articles/PMC37891381#) Interplay of hippocampus and prefrontal cortex in memory. Alison R. Preston, Howard Eichenbaum, Curr Biol., September 9, 2014.

3. Hippocampus: What It Is Function, Location Damage, (https://myclevelandclinic.org/health/body/hippocampus), May 14, 2024.

4. Mild Cognitive Impairment (MCI) (https://mymayoclinic.org/disease-conditions/mild-cognitive-impairment/symptoms-causes/syc-20354578),

October 24, 2024

5. What Is the Hippocampus and What Does It Do? Dan Brennan, MD (https://www.medicinenet.com/what_is_the_hippocampus_and_what_does_it_do/article.htm)

6. Trauma and Post-traumatic Stress disorder modulate polygenic predictors of hippocampal and amygdala volume. (https://www.nature.com/articles/s41398-021-01707-x), Published December 16, 2021. Translational Psychiatry

7. National Library of Medicine National Center for Biotechnology Information (https://pubmed.ncbi.nlm.nih.gov/22054117/#). The hippocampus, neurotrophic factors and depression: possible implications for pharmacotherapy of depression, Gabriel Masi et. al., CNS Drugs, 2011.

8. World Health Organization. Mental Disorders, June 8, 2022 (https://www.who.int/news-room/fact-sheets/detail/mental-disorders#)

9. National Library of Medicine National Center for Biotechnology Information (https://pubmed.ncbi.nlm.gov/22054117/#) The hippocampus, neurotrophic factors and depression: possible implications for the pharmacotherapy of depression, Gabriele Masi et. al., CNS Drugs, 2011

10. Clinical Depression (Major Depressive Disorder): Symptoms. (https://my.clevelandclinic.org/health/disease/24481-clinical-depression-major-depression-disorder). Cleveland Clinic, Last reviewed on 11/30/2022.

11. American Psychiatric Association. What is Depression? (https://www.psychiatry.org//patients-families/depression/What-is-depression). Accessed 11/30/2022.

12. Principles of Trauma Therapy A Guide to Symptoms, Evaluation, and Treatment, John N. Briere, Catherine Scott, 2006.

13. 1 Peter 5:10 (New American Standard Bible)

14. Hebrews 12:2

15. Jeremiah 29:11 (New King James Version)

16. Matthew 5:34 (New International Version)

17. Psalms 34:19 (New King James Version

18. Matthew 27:46

19. Isaiah 53:4 (New American Standard Bible)

20. Pain to Purpose: Mom & Counselor Finds Hope and Purpose The "Big 3" Revealed, Porter, T. (2024).

21. Depression: Dysfunction of Neurons In The

Amygdala May Behind Negative Perceptions Of The Environment. Marianna Alonso, INSTITUT PASTEUR, 10/24/2024. (https://www.pasteur.fr/en/press-area/press-documents/depression-dysfunction-neurons-amygdala-may-be-behind-negative-perceptions-environment#).

22. Isaiah 61:3

23. American Psychiatric Association. (2022). Diagnostic and statistical manual of mental disorders (5th ed., text rev.). American Psychiatric Publishing

24. 2 Timothy 1:7

25. What is psychosocial disability? (https://www.health.nsw.gov.au/mentalhealth/psychosocial/foundations/Pages/psychosocial-whatis.aspx#) February 6, 2023

26. Interpersonal Psychotherapy (IPT): What it is & Techniques. (https://www.myclevelandclinic.org/health/treatments/interpersonal-psychotherapy-ipt), March 6, 2024

27. What is Psychoanalytic Therapy? (https://www.verywellmind.com/whatispsychoanalytictherapy-2795467#) By Kendra Cherry, MSEd | Updated on January 12, 2024. Medically reviewed by Steven Gans, MD

28. National Library of Medicine National Center for Biotechnology Information (https://www.ncbi.nlm.nih.gov/books/NBK606117/#) Psychodynamic Therapy, Caitlin Opland; Tyler J. Torrico, Last Update: September 2, 2024

29. Psychology, Theology, and Spirituality in Christian Counseling. Mark R. McMinn, Ph.D.

30. Numbers 22:28

31. National Library of Medicine National Center for Biotechnology Information (https://www.ncbi.nlm.nih.gov/books/NBK64952/) Chapter 7-Brief Psychodynamic Therapy

32. National Library of Medicine National Center for Biotechnology Information (https://www.ncbi.nlm.nih.gov/books/NBK606117/#) Psychodynamic Therapy, Caitlin Opland; Tyler J. Torrico, Last Update: September 2, 2024

33. Lamentations 3:40 (New International Version)

34. Psalms 139:23-24 (New International Version)

35. Proverbs 4:23 (New Century Version)

36. 2 Corinthians 13:5 (New International Version)

37. Jeremiah 17:10 (New International Version)

38. Jeremiah 29:13 (New King James Version)

Chapter 7: God's Reboot of The Brain

1. Revelation 4:5 (New King James Version)
2. John 4:24
3. Isaiah 66:1
4. NSSL NOAA National Severe Storms Laboratory Severe Weather 101. (https://www.nssl.noaa.gov/education/svrx101/lightning/faq/#).
5. National Weather Service (.gov). Why lightning is beneficial to plants? (https://wwwkztv10.com/weather/sharon's-weather-blog/why-lightning-is-beneficial-to-plants#). Scripps Local Media 2025 Scripps Media Inc.
6. Pasek, M. 2016. Catching lightning in a fossil and calculating how much energy a strike contains. (https://theconversation.com/catching-lightning-in-a-fossil-and-calculating-how-much-energy-a-strike-contains-64152#:)
7. Wikipedia. (https://en.wikipedia.org/wiki/lightning)
8. Wikipedia. (https://en.m.wikipedia.org/wiki/Matter)
9. Robert Matthews, How heavy is electricity? BBC Science Focus. Our Media 2025

(https://www.sciencefocus.com/science/how-heavy-is-electricity).

10. National Weather Service (.gov)

11. The Sound of Thunder. https://www.weather.gov/source/Zhu/ZHU_Training_Page/lightning2/thunderstorm.html

12. Understanding Sound, (https://www.nps.gov/subject/sound/understandingsouds.htm).

13. Isaiah 45:18 (New King James Version)

14. https://www.nps.gov

15. Ephesians 2:6

16. National Library of Medicine Plus Trusted Health Information for you. What is a cell? (https://medlineplus.gov/genetics/understanding/basics/cell/#). Last Updated February 2021.

17. Wikipedia (https://en.m.wikipedia.org/wiki/Atom)

18. Composition of the Human Body, Wikipedia. (https://en.m.wikipedia.org/wiki/composition_of_the_human_body).

19. Genesis 2:7 (New King James Version)

20. Genesis 1:1-2 (New King James Version)

21. Revelation 1:8 (New King James Version)

22. Alpha Wave (https://sciencedirect.com/topics/neuroscience/alpha-wave)

23. Brain Waves (https://www.sciencedirect.com/topics/agriculture-and-biological-sciences/brain-waves).

24. What are alpha brain waves? Plus 5 benefits of increasing them. Clinically Reviewed by Dr. Chris Mosunic, PhD, RD, MBA. (https://www.calm.com/blog/alpha-brain-waves#).

25. What is AED? (https://www.redcross.org/take-a-class/aed/using-an-aed/what-is-aed).

26. Rhythm, Wikipedia (https://en.m.wikipedia.org/wiki/Rythm).

27. Estes P. MS1, The Mediating Effects of Prayer on the Anterior Cingulate Cortex's Regulation of Anxiety (https://journals.indianapolis.iu.edu/index.php/insight/article/download/27477/25033/53946#).

28. Shinya Fuji, Catherine Y. Wan, The Role of Rhythm in Speech and Language Rehabilitation: The SEP Hypothesis. National Library of Medicine National Center for Biotechnology Information. (https://pmc.ncbi.nlm.nih.gov/articles/pmc41952751/#). Frontiers in Human Neuroscience. October 13, 2014

29. Romans 8:26

30. Galatians 5:22

31. Romans 8:26 (New King James Version)

32. 1 Corinthians 14:4 (New King James Version)

33. Luke 24:49 (New King James Version)

34. Romans 8:9 (New King James Version)

35. 1 Corinthians 14:28

36. Jeremiah 20:9 (New King James Version)

37. Cardiac Conduction System, Medically Reviewed on 1/7/2025. (https://my.clevelandclinic.org/health/today/22562-electrical-system-of-the-heart).

38. Explainer: How cells use chemistry to make the electricity of life, By Bethany Brookshire, (https://www.snexplores.org/article/ion-chemistry-cell-electricity#).

39. Eunice Kennedy Shriver, What are the parts of the nervous system? National Institute of Child Health and Human Development. (https://www.nichd.nih.gov/health/topics/neuro/conditioninfo/parts). Office of Communications. Last Reviewed Date 10/1/2018.

40. Julia Layton & Mark Mancini, How Does the Body Make Electricity-and How Does it Use it? (https://www.health.howstuffworks.com/human

-body/systems/nervous-system/human-body-make-electricity.htm#). Updated: August 1, 2022.

41. Nerves. Cleveland Clinic (https://my.clevelandclinic.org/health/body/22584-nerves), 2025.

42. How The Heart Works. How The Heart Beats, National Heart, Lung, and Blood Institute (https://www.nhlbi.nih.gov/health/heart/heart-beats#).

43. Brain-to-brain communication: the possible role of brain electromagnetic fields (As a Potential Hypothesis) Ehsan Hosseini (https://www.sciencedirect.com/science/article/pii/s2405844021004680#) March 2021, Heliyon

44. M Bruce Maclver, Consciousness and inward electromagnetic field interactions, National Library of Medicine National Center for Biotechnology Information (https://pmc.ncbi.nlm.nih.gov/articles/PMC9714613/#) November 17, 2022. Front Hum Neurosci.

45. EEG (electroencephalogram) EEG brain activity by Mayo Clinic Staff (https://www.mayoclinic.org/tests-procedures/eeg/about/pac-20393875#) May 29, 2024.

46. A Picture-Perfect Look at How Electrical

Activity Travels through the Brain. New imaging technique developed by BU, MIT researchers can detect individual brain cells firing in the brain then ever before. By Ann Trafton, (https://www.bu.edu/articles/2019/how-electricity-activity-travels-through-the brain/#) October 10, 2019. Neuroscience. The Brink.

47. Hebrews 3:15 (English Standard Version)

48. John 10:27 (New International Version)

49. Luke 8:11-12

50. Revelation 4:5

51. Isaiah 11:2

52. James 1:22 (New King James Version)

53. John 1:1 (New Kings James Version)

54. Genesis 1

55. Genesis 1:2

56. Genesis 1:26

57. Isaiah 55:11 (New King James Version)

58. Job 22:28-29

59. Revelation 1:6

60. Romans 4:17

61. What Brain Science Tells Us About Religious Belief, by Tom Rosentiel, Pew Research Center

(https://www.pewresearch.org/science/2008/05/05what-brain-science-tells-us-about-religous-belief/) May 5, 2008.

62. How Faith and Prayer Benefit the Brain by Gayle D. Beebe, PhD (https://www.westmont.edu/how-faith-and-prayer-benefit-the-brain) President Westmont Magazine, Spring 2012.

63. How Prayer Rewires the Brain, By Elizabeth and Joy Schmus (https://www.prayer/leader.com/how-prayer-rewires-the-brain), Church Prayer Leader Network, 2025.

64. Electric Circuits-Lesson 2-Electrical Current Requirements of a Circuit. (https://www.physicsclassroom.com/class/circuits/Lesson-2/Requirements-of-a-Circuit#). The Physics Classroom, 2025.

65. John 17:16

66. Matthew 6:10

67. Ephesians 2:8

68. 1 Peter 1:16 (New King James Version)

69. Traumatic Stress: effects on the brain, J. Douglas Bremner, National Library of Medicine National Center for Biotechnology Information, (https://pmc.ncbi.nlm.nih.gov/articles/PMC3181836/#). December 8, 2006.

70. Psalms 46:10

71. Grounding Techniques for Post-Traumatic Stress Disorder, Why using your senses can help you cope. By Matthew Tull, PhD (https://www.verywellmind.com/grounding-techniques-for-ptsd-2797300#:). Updated on August 16, 2024. Medically Reviewed by Amy Morin, LCSW.

72. Isaiah 26:3 (New Living Translation)

73. Mind-Body Interactions and Mindfulness Meditation in Diabetes. Gagan Priya, Sanjay Kalra. National Library of Medicine National Center for Biotechnology Information. (https://pmc.ncbi.nlm.nih.gov/articles/PMC5954593/). April 18, 2018.

74. Effectiveness of a mindful nature walking intervention on sleep quality and mood in university students during Covid-19: A randomized control study. Jingni Ma, Joanne M. Williams, Paul Graham Morris, Stella Wy Chan. National Library of Medicine National Center of Biotechnology Information. (https://pmc.ncbi.nlm.nih.gov/articles/PMC9365743/) August 11, 2022. Pub Med Central.

75. Psalms 63:6 (King James Version)

76. Psalms 77:12 (King James Version)

77. Psalms 143:5 (King James Version)

Chapter 8: God's Reformat and New Design

1. Revelation 21:5 (New King James Version)
2. How To Format A Hard Drive, Ruth Rowley (https://www.overclockers.co.uk/blog/how-to-format-a-hard-drive/#). October 12, 2023, OverlockersUK. Gaming. Gaming Hardware
3. John 10:10
4. Isaiah 43:19 (New King James Version)
5. Luke 10:10
6. Neural Plasticity: 4 Steps to change your Brain & Habits, Dr. Kim, Dr. Hilery, Authenticity Associates Coaching & Counseling (https://www.authenticityassociates.com/neural-plasticity-4-steps-to-change-your-brain/#). June 21, 2010.
7. Romans 12:2
8. Philippians 4:8 (New King James Version)
9. Beck, Judith S. 2020. Cognitive Behavior Therapy. 3rd ed. London, England
10. Global Research Pattern of Cognitive Distortion: A Bibliometric Analysis, Fauziah Zaiden, Mastura Mahfar, Faizah Mohd Fakhruddin. (https://journals.sagepub.com/doi/10./177/21582440231219658?icid=int.sj-abstract.citing-articles.9). December 24, 2023. Sage Journals.

2025

11. Types of Parenting Styles and Effects on Children, Terrence Sandvictores; Magda D. Mendez. National Library of Medicine, National Center for Biotechnology Information. (https://www.ncbi.nlm.nih.gov/books/NBK568743/#). September 18, 2012.

12. American Psychiatric Association. (2022). Diagnostic and statistical manual of mental disorders (5th ed., text rev.). American Psychiatric Publishing

13. Colossians 1:13

14. 1 Corinthians 2:16

15. John 16:13

16. 2 Corinthians 10:5

17. Song of Solomon 2:15

18. John 15:5

19. Proverbs 4:23

20. Jeremiah 17:9 (New King James Version)

21. Ephesians 5:26

22. Psalms 51:10

23. Beck, J.S. (2021), Cognitive Behavior Therapy: Basics and Beyond (3rd ed.). The Gilford Press. Beck, A.T., (1963). Burns, D.D., (1980).

24. John 15:1

25. Luke 9:23 (New King James Version)

26. Proverbs 21:2-3

27. Proverbs 16:9

28. John 10:10 (New Living Translation)

Chapter 9: Hope and Healing

1. Hebrews 6:19 (New King James Version)
2. Ephesians 3:20 (New King James Version)
3. Pain to Purpose: Mom & Counselor Finds Hope and Purpose The “Big 3” Revealed, Porter, T. (2024).
4. 1 Corinthians 15:55-57
5. Psalms 34:18
6. 2 Corinthians 12:9 (New King James Version)
7. 2 Corinthians 1:20
8. 2 Chronicles 20:15
9. Isaiah 52:12
10. Psalms 121:1
11. 1 Timothy 6:12
12. Proverbs 3:5-6 (New King James Version)
13. 2 Timothy 1:7 (New King James Version)

14. Philippians 3:14 (King James Version)
15. James 1:2-4
16. Galatians 5:22-23 (New King James Version)
17. 1 John 4:18 (New King James Version)
18. John 15:13 (New King James Version)
19. Job 1:21 (New King James Version)
20. Ephesians 6:10
21. Ephesians 6:13-17
22. Hebrews 3:13
23. Proverbs 27:17 (New King James Version)
24. Genesis 1:28
25. Galatians 5:22-23
26. Colossians 1:27
27. Revelation 12:11
28. 1 Peter 4:13 (New King James Version)
29. Romans 8:17 (New King James Version)
30. Romans 8:18 (New King James Version)
31. Romans 8:19 (New King James Version)
32. Romans 8:20 (New King James Version)
33. Hebrews 11:1 (New King James Version)

34. Psalms 138:8

35. Romans 8:25 (New King James Version)

36. Hebrews 6:20

37. John 16:33 (New King James Version)

38. Pain to Purpose: Mom & Counselor Finds Hope and Purpose The "Big 3" Revealed, Porter, T. (2024).

39. Romans 8:28 (New King James Version)

40. Isaiah 54:17 (New King James Version)

41. Romans 8:29-30

42. Romans 8:31

43. Galatians 6:9-10

44. Philippians 3:14 (New King James Version)

45. Galatians 6:9

46. Pain to Purpose: Mom & Counselor Finds Hope and Purpose The "Big 3" Revealed, Porter, T. (2024).

47. Psalms 23:4 (New King James Version)

48. Genesis 1:27

49. Isaiah 53:3-5

50. Isaiah 53:3

51. Pain to Purpose: Mom & Counselor Finds Hope

and Purpose The "Big 3" Revealed, Porter, T. (2024).

52. Psalms 51:10 (New King James Version)

53. Psalms 51:12 (New King James Version)

54. Psalms 43:2

55. Psalms 18:1-2

56. Philippians 4:7

57. Pain to Purpose: Mom & Counselor Finds Hope and Purpose The "Big 3" Revealed, Porter, T. (2024).

58. Job 13:15 (New King James Version)

59. Matthew 11:12 (New King James Version)

Chapter 10: Jesus, The Wonderful Counselor

1. Matthew 11:28 (New King James Version)

2. Isaiah 55:9 (New King James Version)

3. Psalms 119-105 (New King James Version)

4. Galatians 3:13-14

5. Lating, M. J., and Everly Jr., S., George. A Clinical Guide to the Treatment of the Human Stress Response (3rd ed.). (Springer New York, 2012).

6. Brier, J.N., Scott, C. Principles of Trauma Therapy A Guide To Symptoms, Evaluation,

And Treatment (2nd ed.). (SAGE Publications, Inc., 2014).

7. Cohen, A. Judith, Mannarino, P., Anthony, Deblinger, E. Treating Trauma and Traumatic Grief in Children and Adolescents (2nd ed.)
8. Revelation 22:18 (New King James Version)
9. Proverbs 1:31 (New International Version)
10. Cohen, A. Judith, Mannarino, P., Anthony, Deblinger, E. Treating Trauma and Traumatic Grief in Children and Adolescents (2nd ed.)
11. Matthew 6:34 (New Living Translation)
12. Codependency: Signs, Causes, and Help for a Co-dependent Relationship. By Sheldon Reid, Reviewed by Tatiana Rivera Cruz, LICSW. Love & Friendship. (https://www.helpguide.org/relationships/social-connection/codependencey)
13. Isaiah 2:22 (New Living Translation)
14. Exodus 34:14 (New King James Version)
15. Matthew 6:24 (New International Version)
16. Revelation 3:15-16 (New King James Version)
17. Psalms 146:3-4 (New International Version)
18. James 1:5 (New International Version)
19. Proverbs 1:7 (New International Version)

20. Hebrews 12:1 (New Living Translation)

21. Ephesians 5:27 (New King James Version)

22. Ephesians 5:25-26 (New International Version)

23. Matthew 22:36-39 (New International Version)

24. 1 Corinthians 13:4-8 (New King James Version-The Care and Counsel Bible)

25. John 13:34-35 (New International Version)

26. 1 Corinthians 13:1-7

27. Healthy Relationships (https://www.thejenmoff.com)

28. James 1:9 (New Living Translation)

29. James 2:14-17 (New Living Translation)

30. Romans 16:20 (New International Version)

Appendix B:

1. Felitti, V.J., Anda, R.F., Nordenberg, D., Williamson, D.F., Spitz, A.M., Edwards, V., Koss, M.P., & Marks, J.S. (1998) and Anda, R.F., Fleisher, V.J., Edwards, V.J., Whitfield, C.L., Dube, S.R., Williamson, D.F. (2004) Adverse Childhood Experiences (ACE's).

Appendix C:

1. American Psychiatric Association. (2022). Diagnostic and statistical manual of mental

disorders (5th ed., text rev.). American Psychiatric Publishing.

Appendix D:

1. Langley, J. N. (1903). The autonomic nervous system. Brain, 26(4), 616-96
2. Langley, J.N. (1903). The autonomic nervous system. Cambridge, Heffer.
3. Porges, S.W. (2011). The polyvagal theory: Neurophysiological foundations of emotions attachment, communication, and self-regulation. W.W. Norton Company.
4. Porges, S.W. (2018). Polyvagal Theory: A primer. In S.W. Porges & D. Dana (Eds), Clinical applications of the polyvagal theory: The emergence of polyvagal-informed therapies (pp.50-69). W.W. Norton & Company.

About The Author

Tina Porter is the Founder and Owner of Inspire Hope Counseling Ministry Center, LLC, a Christ-Centered and Faith-based Professional Counseling Ministry and Private Practice that provides biblical, spiritual, pastoral, grief, trauma, mental health, crisis response, marriage and family counseling services, and professional mental health coaching for individuals, couples, and families.

Tina Porter earned a Master of Arts Degree in Human Services Counseling: Crisis Response and Trauma, earned a Bachelor of Science Degree in Social Work. Tina also completed Regional and National Clinical Certification Training in Trauma Focused Cognitive Behavioral Therapy (TFCBT) and Trauma-focused therapies. She has completed extensive clinical training in Grief, Trauma, and Mental Health Counseling. Tina is a Qualified Mental Health Professional (QMHP) having worked in the mental health field for 29 years. Tina Porter is now the Founder and Owner of a faith-based private practice and ministry. She integrates psychological psychotherapy and the Christian Faith, serving as a Christian Counselor and Therapist, Minister, Pastoral Counselor, and Spiritual Leader providing pastoral counseling at her church, for the church as a whole, for professionals, first responders, medical professionals, ministers, church leaders, pastors, and community members.

Tina has supervised and overseen various trauma, crisis, and grief-based programs at various agencies. She has worked as a Mental Health Counselor at various mental health and behavioral health agencies. Tina was previously employed for a Hospice Agency as a Hospice Medical Social Worker and Grief Counselor and Bereavement Coordinator for 7 years, working closely with Chaplains. Solely, a Christian Counseling Provider, and a member of the American Association of Christian Counselors, (AACC), Tina utilizes her 29 years, and in counting, education, experience, clinical training, administrative leadership, and expertise in the mental health and human services field to serve the Church, Community, Region, and Nation. As a Pastor/Minister currently serving in ministry with more than 23 years of experience in many capacities of ministry in various churches, Tina integrates psychological therapy, with Christian theology, spirituality, prayer, and Biblical truths in her practice and ministry.

Tina Porter, and her husband, Aaron J. Porter Sr. are also Founders and Owners of The Aaron Joseph Porter Jr. AP3 Hope Foundation, Inc., a Private Owned Family Legacy Foundation with a charitable mission to provide immediate hardship assistance and aid to grieving parents and families, and to student-athletes who have lost a fellow teammate. Additionally, The AP3 Hope Foundation, Inc. provides annual AP3 Legacy Scholarships to student-athletes.

Tina Porter, grounded in God, faith, and prayer, is a sought-after public speaker, and minister who conducts inspirational, professional, ministry trainings, church conferences, church services, and motivational speaking engagements to do what she does best: to spread the message of *Hope* and to *Inspire Hope* to one person at a time and around the world. Recently, Tina appeared on **TCT (Total Christian Television) TV Network on TCT Today**, **Small Town and Big Business Podcast**, and **The Prime Marriage Podcast** as a guest appearance to share her professional expertise, Christian faith, her story of Tragedy to Triumph following the loss of her beloved son in 2018, Inspire Hope Counseling Ministry

Center, LLC, AP3 Hope Foundation, Inc. and her book, ***Pain to Purpose: Counselor and Mom finds Hope and Purpose-The "Big 3" Revealed* that was released on September 29, 2024.**

You can connect with Tina via email and direct messaging through her social media pages. Tina invites you to follow her on all her social media pages, listed below. You can also connect to Tina by visiting her website: www.inspirehopeministry.org

Email: inspirehopemin@icloud.com

Facebook: @ Inspire Hope Counseling Ministry Center, LLC

www.facebook.com/InspireHopeCounselingMinistryCenterLLC

@ AP3 Hope Foundation Inc.

www.facebook.com/AP3HopeFoundationInc

Instagram: @ap3hopefoundation

www.instagram.com/ap3hopefoundation

Inspire Hope

COUNSELING MINISTRY CENTER, LLC

*Inspiring student athletes to strive
for greatness and run their race.*

Find Hope and Purpose

Best Print Seller that has impacted thousands around the globe on how to find meaning, peace, hope, and purpose as Tina Porter, author, founder, and owner of Inspire Hope Counseling Ministry Center, LLC, and AP3 Hope Foundation, Inc. as well as trauma, grief, and mental health expert, and pastor offers guidance to embrace hope as a beacon of light to lead you on the path of finding purpose in the darkness of pain!

Connect with TINA PORTER

Visit: **www.inspirehopeministry.org**

to learn more about Tina Porter and her Ministry, Counseling Business, Guest Appearances on TCT Today, The Prime Marriage Podcast, Small Town Big Business Podcast, and as Speaker for Illinois College Association (ICCCSSO) Professional Training, Panelist Speaker for SIU Foundation Saluki Women's Weekend Women in Empowerment Conference etc.

Also follow her on social media.

Facebook: www.facebook.com/

InspireHopeCounselingMinistryCenterLLC

www.ingramcontent.com/pod-product-compliance
Lightning Source LLC
Chambersburg PA
CBHW071713120626
46550CB00001B/216
* 9 7 9 8 2 1 8 7 6 2 3 9 1 *